The Editor

John Greenleaf Whittier

THE SUPERNATURALISM
OF NEW ENGLAND

JOHN GREENLEAF WHITTIER

THE
SUPERNATURALISM
OF NEW ENGLAND

Edited, and with an Introduction,

by

EDWARD WAGENKNECHT

NORMAN
UNIVERSITY OF OKLAHOMA PRESS

LIBRARY OF CONGRESS CATALOG CARD NUMBER: 69–10628

Copyright 1969 by the University of Oklahoma Press, Publishing Division of the University. Composed and printed at Norman, Oklahoma, U.S.A., by the University of Oklahoma Press. First Edition.

CONTENTS

v

EDITOR'S INTRODUCTION

EDITOR'S INTRODUCTION

BY ANY STRICT DEFINITION of the term, John Greenleaf Whittier could no more have qualified as a folklorist than as an historian, but this could hardly have been expected of a man who began working with the floating traditions of New England before the word "folklore" had even been coined and nearly half a century before the English Folklore Society was established. When Whittier published his first book, *Legends of New England*, in 1831, the first edition of the *Kinder- und Hausmärchen* of the Brothers Grimm was only nineteen years old and the *Deutsche Mythologie* yet four years in the future. His "Narrative and Legendary Poems" stand together in his collected works, with no differentiation made between materials derived from native and foreign sources nor between history and superstition. When he dealt with actualities, as in "Barbara Frietchie" and "Skipper Ireson's Ride," he was rarely accurate (no more was Longfellow in "Paul Revere's Ride" and "The Wreck of the Hesperus"), for though his literary theory may not have been very involved or sophisticated, he was always intelligent enough to know that a creative writer

3

is supposed to be just that, and that there is no point in having been endowed with an imagination unless you plan to make use of it. And if this absolved him, as a poet, from the obligations which rested upon the historian and the biographer, in his day as in ours, it excused him all the more from those now imposed upon the scientific student of folklore, for this is a creature of whose existence neither he nor many of the persons who were alive at the beginning of his career could well have dreamed.

Whittier was not accurate even about his own ancestry, and Whitman Bennett remarked of the *Legends of New England*:

> It is amusing to note that he is not absolutely accurate as to his facts, even when he names the two Indians who first appeared at Plymouth in the spring of 1621, being just half right and half wrong, for all through life he had the habit of never being quite exact, twisting the facts of legends or events he commemorated. In his preface, he says that he shall have accomplished his purpose if the book inspires further investigation and recording of New England antiquities, which have been sadly neglected. And here again he is not quite right, for [Samuel G.] Drake and [Charles W.] Upham had already begun their researches and publications.[1]

Upham's *Lectures on Witchcraft* came out the year after *Legends* and Drake's *Book of the Indians* one year later, but the latter's *Antiquities of Boston* was not to appear until 1856, and his *Annals of Witchcraft in the United States* not before 1869. Whittier was an avid reader of such books

[1] *Whittier, Bard of Freedom* (University of North Carolina Press, 1941).

when he could get hold of them. He called Alonzo Lewis's *History of Lynn* (1829) his source for the long poem, *Moll Pitcher,* which was published the same year as the *Legends,* and Cecil B. Williams's study of "The Historicity of *Leaves from Margaret Smith's Journal*"[2] abundantly documented his knowledge both of the Colonial writers and of contemporary scholarship in Colonial history.

Whether Joshua Coffin, the schoolmaster who so effectively introduced (or reintroduced) Whittier to Robert Burns, exercised as important an influence in directing the young poet's attention to the investigation of his Essex County backgrounds as Theodore Roosevelt Garrison thinks[3] is doubtful, for Garrison himself admits that we do not know how far Coffin's later well-known interest in local history had developed by the time he and Whittier came together. But we have the poet's own word for it that his discovery of Burns turned him away from the Gothicism and rootless romanticism that had hitherto enthralled him, and for this alone we are all greatly in Coffin's debt.

[2] Ph.D. dissertation, University of Chicago, 1933. The University Libraries published Chapter IV in pamphlet form in 1936.

[3] In his Ph.D. dissertation, "John Greenleaf Whittier, Pioneer Regionalist and Folklorist" (University of Wisconsin, 1960), now available through University Microfilms. There are two other dissertations bearing upon the points under consideration in this book: Harry Oster, "Whittier and Folklore," Cornell University (M.A.), 1950, and George Gibson Carey, "Folklore in the Writings of John Greenleaf Whittier," Indiana University, Ph.D., 1966. I have not seen Oster's dissertation, though Carey makes use of it. I wish to acknowledge the kindness of Dr. Carey in lending me a copy of his work. Though I have taken no quotations from either Carey or Garrison, I have read both with profit, and they have contributed to my general knowledge of the subjects discussed.

New light on home-seen Nature beamed,
    New glory over Woman;
And daily life and duty seemed
    No longer poor and common.

I woke to find the simple truth
    Of fact and feeling better
Than all the dreams that held my youth
    A still repining debtor:

That Nature gives her handmaid, Art,
    The themes of sweet discoursing;
The tender idyls of the heart
    In every tongue rehearsing.

Why dream of lands of gold and pearl,
    Of loving knight and lady,
When farmer boy and barefoot girl
    Were wandering there already?

To be sure, the line of development was not nearly so
straight in life as it can be made to appear on paper. (It
seldom is.) One would suppose, for example, that Whittier's familiarity with the work of the minor New Hampshire Burns, Robert Dinsmore or Dinsmoor (1757–1836),
with whom he shared the glory of the opening exercises at
Haverhill Academy in 1827, and about whom he wrote an
essay in *Old Portraits and Modern Sketches* (1850), must
have reinforced the Burns-induced tendency to turn for
literary material to the world around him, and speaking
generally it may well have done so, but it is discouraging to
find him writing in Scottish dialect because Dinsmore had
done so! There was nothing to mislead him, on the other

hand, in the work of the Connecticut poet, John G. C. Brainard (1796–1828), whose *Literary Remains* he had edited the year before the *Legends* appeared. Not only did he quote Brainard on the title page of the *Legends*, but a good deal of the material in the volume derives from him or is based upon stories which he had already used.

Though Whittier attributes some of his material in the *Legends* and elsewhere to oral sources, I am sure it would be safe to say that, generally speaking, he derived much more from printed records. Nevertheless he often used, without independent checking, items sent to him by various correspondents; thus Mrs. E. D. E. N. Southworth gave him what became "Barbara Frietchie." It might also be well to remember that he had an uncle who once saw three hags circling about a caldron in a forest clearing and that the apparition of his aunt's lover rode up to her home in Massachusetts at the exact time of his death in New York. It may well be that the conditioning or determination of Whittier's attitudes by such circumstances was basically more important than any study of percentages could show. In the last analysis, he may very well have become the man and writer he was because as a boy he belonged to the circle which gathered about the hearth on winter evenings in the charming old farmhouse near Haverhill, which now stands, open to all Americans, unhaunted by any ghosts save that of a better America than any we now possess.

> Our mother, while she turned her wheel
> Or run the new-knit stocking-heel,
> Told how the Indian hordes came down
> At midnight on Cocheco town,
> And how her own great-uncle bore

His cruel scalp-mark to fourscore.
Recalling, in her fitting phrase,
   So rich and picturesque and free,
   (The common unrhymed poetry
Of simple life and country ways,)
The story of her early days,—
She made us welcome to her home;
Old hearths grew wide to give us room;
We stole with her a frightened look
At the gray wizard's conjuring-book,
The fame whereof went far and wide
Through all the simple country side;
We heard the hawks at twilight play,
The boat-horn on Piscataqua,
The loon's weird laughter far away;
We fished her little trout-brook, knew
What flowers in wood and meadow grew,
What sunny hillsides autumn-brown
She climbed to shake the ripe nuts down,
Saw where in sheltered cove and bay
The ducks' black squadron anchored lay,
And heard the wild-geese calling loud
Beneath the gray November cloud.

Legends of New England was reprinted, with an introduction by John B. Pickard, by Scholars' Facsimiles and
Reprints, in 1965, but *The Supernaturalism of New England* has never until now been reprinted in its entirety since
it first appeared, under the imprint of Wiley and Putnam,
in New York and London, in January, 1847. Under the title
"New England Supernaturalism," some of it had already
been published in the September, October, and November
numbers of the *United States Magazine and Democratic
Review* during the year 1843. As "Charms and Fairy Faith,"

8

"Magicians and Witch Folk," and "The Agency of Evil," portions of it reappeared in Whittier's *Literary Recreations and Miscellanies* in 1854 and subsequently in the collected works. According to the standard bibliographer Currier, the "Dedication" was the first printing anywhere of the poem later called "To My Sister," and portions of "The Burial of Pennacook" represented the first printing in book form. "The New Wife and the Old," which is quoted by Whittier, had already been printed several times.

With *The Supernaturalism of New England* I have included between these covers, in Appendix A, a paper on "New England Superstitions," which first appeared in the *New England Magazine,* July, 1833, and which at least serves to show that Whittier had collected some of the material he used in *Supernaturalism* as early as 1833, ten years before any of it appeared in serial form and fourteen years before the book came out.[4] In Appendix B, I have reprinted Hawthorne's severe review of the *Supernaturalism,* not only because it shows one of the leading New England writers reviewing another but because it raises fundamental questions and thus helps us to understand Whittier better.

Hawthorne, as the reader will observe, criticizes Whittier, first, for a certain pretentiousness, and, next, for what he regards as a shallow rationalism and lack of imagination. He sees no reason for believing that contact with the Indians modified the superstitions and folk beliefs which the colonists brought over from England, nor that there was such a thing as a distinctively New England brand of supernaturalism, though he is not perhaps quite consistent on this

[4] This has been previously reprinted by Edwin H. Cady and Harry Hayden Clark in their *Whittier on Writers and Writing* (Syracuse University Press, 1950). I follow the Cady–Clark text.

9

last point when he goes on to attribute certain assumed qualities of New England character to New England ghosts. But what really annoys him is that Whittier condescends too much, stooping to his theme "with the austere dignity of a schoolmaster at his amusements," or that, in other words, he fails to achieve what Coleridge described as "that willing suspension of disbelief for a moment which constitutes poetic faith." "If he cannot believe his ghost-story while he is telling it, he had better leave the task to somebody else."

Was Hawthorne's a fair criticism? There is, I think, a good deal to be said on his side of the argument. Whittier does seem overanxious to guard against the danger that, in writing about superstition, he shall himself be deemed superstitious, and he rarely tells a story without (often awkwardly) going out of his way to indicate that he does not believe it, or at least that he does not require the reader to do so. It may be objected that Hawthorne himself often does the same thing, but the criticism will not hold. Hawthorne does it only in fiction (his factual accounts of the ghost of Dr. Harris in the Boston Athenaeum and the ghosts at the Old Manse and the Mall Street house in Salem are straightforward enough), and he does it quite differently, using ambivalence as both an aspect of his literary technique and an expression of his conception of the nature of life itself: characteristically he offers the reader a choice between a natural and a preternatural explanation of a phenomenon, refraining from committing himself or from pressing either belief or disbelief upon anybody else, but insisting that each reader judge for himself and judge himself also by his choice.

Whittier, among other things, suggests that superstitions

thrive because priests and other agents of the establishment keep them alive for interested motives, and that psychics get their occasionally impressive results through a shrewd knowledge of the character of the people they are dealing with. Sometimes he seems out-and-out materialistic, as when he states bluntly that a fresh coat of paint on a haunted house serves as the best form of exorcism, and when no other explanation will serve he may even suggest that matters which puzzle us now may be understood better in time to come as the expression of some physical law which we have not yet apprehended. On the other hand, he tells us that he would rather swallow all the superstitions that have ever attached themselves to all the faiths of men than be left without God in the world; in the ordinary sense of the term, Whittier was certainly a more devout man than Hawthorne himself. What, then, are the real reasons for what seems a somewhat excessive scepticism in this book? The explanation is not single, but I think it is still fairly clear.

To begin with, it is clear that Whittier's inborn romanticism responded intensely to the folk beliefs to which he was so abundantly exposed from his infancy. His literary tastes in early life were distinctly Gothic, and his early writings involve much violence and garish supernaturalism. Later, long after he had left much of this behind him, he read the reports of the Society for Psychical Research with care and (like Thomas Hardy) greatly regretted his inability to see a ghost.

It must not be forgotten, however, that, religious as Whittier was, he rejected a great many things that most of his religiously-minded countrymen accepted. To begin with, he was a Quaker, and this meant that churchianity was nothing to him. Quakers have no priest, no sacraments, no formulated creed. They revere the Bible but regard the Inner Light in the believer's own soul as the ultimate authority. Whittier personally rejected the Second Coming of Christ (in which there was widespread interest in his day); though not a universalist, he refused to believe that probation ended with this life; he was undismayed by either the new science or the new Biblical criticism, because his faith, based upon mystical apprehension of God, did not rest ultimately upon any witness that could be invalidated by such studies.

> We may not climb the heavenly steeps
>   To bring the Lord Christ down;
> In vain we search the lowest deeps,
>   For Him no depths can drown.
>
> Nor holy bread, nor blood of grape,
>   The lineaments restore
> Of Him we know in outward shape
>   And in the flesh no more.
>
> He cometh not a king to reign;
>   The world's long hope is dim;
> The weary centuries watch in vain
>   The clouds of heaven for Him.
>
> Death comes, life goes; the asking eye
>   And ear are answerless;
> The grave is dumb, the hollow sky
>   Is sad with silentness.
>
> The letter fails, and systems fall,
>   And every symbol wanes;

The Spirit over-brooding all
　　Eternal Love remains.

And not for signs in heaven above
　　Or earth below they look,
Who know with John His smile of love,
　　With Peter His rebuke.

If religious faith was to survive into the coming age, Whittier was firmly convinced that the old false foundations must be torn out from under it and the new sure foundation of the testimony of the soul itself built in.

He did not wish to be dogmatic about any of this, but he does not compromise on any essential issue. As he says in the work we have here under consideration, he had always had trouble in deciding where faith ends and fanaticism begins. Both as a Quaker and as a Christian, he eschewed both sectarianism and exclusivism ("other sheep I have which are not of this fold"); wherever men had reached out toward God, through any means, was for him a sacred spot, and he was sure that God's ear was sympathetically attuned toward Christian and "heathen" alike. He would have sympathized completely with the reply which Dickens made to the American advocate of slavery who inquired whether he did not believe that the Bible sanctioned it; Dickens said that he did not, but that if he could be convinced that it did, he would reject the Bible also. On the other hand, I am sure Whittier would have been horrified by John Wesley's reputed judgment that if belief in witchcraft were overthrown, Christianity would go with it. To him it seemed, on the contrary, that if Christianity ever did die out, it would be the idiotic superstitions which had been allowed to attach themselves to it that destroyed it, and if you had asked him how he could be sure that men who abandoned superstition would not go on to reject faith also, I fancy he might have asked you how you supposed a mother was able to pour out the bath water without pouring out the baby with it.

The essential point of the matter, of course, is that Whittier's God was a God of Love, whose essential nature had been revealed to men supremely in Jesus Christ.

> I know not where His islands lift
>   Their fronded palms in air;
> I only know I cannot drift
>   Beyond His love and care.

If it ever occurred to him that a fundamentally spiritual universe might conceivably include horrors which a purely material world could not encompass, he must surely have put the thought away from him as a species of blasphemy. No belief which inspired such inhumanity as had been inspired by the belief in witchcraft could conceivably be sound or in harmony with God's will, and though he says nothing about the matter in detail, he makes it clear in his introduction to *The Supernaturalism of New England* itself that one reason why he must be so uncompromising in his treatment of superstition was that he did not wish to share the responsibility for causing others to bear the burden of the superstitious terrors which he himself had experienced as a child before he had reasoned out his mature position on such matters.

Though his expression of it may be more devout, Whittier's essential attitude toward religion was not, therefore, very different from that of James Russell Lowell in the greatest religious poem written by any of the standard New England writers of the nineteenth century, *The Cathedral*.

Nothing that keeps thought out is safe from thought.
For there's no virgin-fort but self-respect,
And Truth defensive hath lost hold on God.

                     . . . be He nowhere else,
God is in all that liberates and lifts,
In all that humbles, sweetens, and consoles.

This life were brutish did we not sometimes
Have intimation clear of wider scope,
Hints of occasion infinite, to keep
The soul alert with noble discontent
And onward yearning of unstilled desire;
Fruitless, except we now and then divined
A mystery of Purpose, gleaming through
The secular confusions of the world,
Whose will we darkly accomplish, doing ours.
No man can think nor in himself perceive,
Sometimes at waking, in the street sometimes,
Or on the hillside, always unforewarned,
A grace of being, finer than himself,
That beckons and is gone,—a larger life
Upon his own impinging, with swift glimpse
Of spacious circles luminous with mind,
To which the ethereal substance of his own
Seems but gross cloud to make that visible,
Touched to a sudden glory round the edge.
Who that hath known these visitations fleet
Would strive to make them trite and ritual?

15

And if there is an incompleteness about modern religion, as there may well be, this only brings it closer to life itself, of which the same thing is true.

> I fear not Thy withdrawal; more I fear,
> Seeing, to know Thee not, hoodwinked with dreams
> Of signs and wonders, while, unnoticed, Thou,
> Walking Thy garden still, commun'st with men,
> Missed in the commonplace of miracle.

Whittier also comes close to Lowell in the famous 1868 essay on "Witchcraft" in the latter's *Among My Books.* Ghosts, like witches, are as romantic as fairies for those who do not believe in them, but they are stern realism for those who do, and it may be that Whittier would never have been able to enjoy New England supernaturalism as much as he did without first having freed himself from the terror of belief.

> Credulity [wrote Lowell], as a mental and moral phenomenon, manifests itself in widely different ways, according as it chances to be the daughter of fancy or terror. The one lies warm about the heart as Folk-lore, fills moonlit dells with dancing fairies, sets out a meal for the Brownie, hears the tinkle of airy bridle-bells as Tamlane rides away with the Queen of Dreams, changes Pluto and Proserpine into Oberon and Titania, and makes friends with unseen powers as Good Folk; the other is a bird of night, whose shadow sends a chill among the roots of the hair; it sucks with the vampire, gorges with the ghoul, is choked by the night-hag, pines away under the witch's charm, and commits uncleanness with the embodied Principle of Evil, giving up the fair realm of

innocent belief to a murky throng from the slums and stews of the debauched brain. Both have vanished from among educated men, and such superstition as comes to the surface nowadays is the harmless Jacobitism of sentiment, pleasing itself with a fiction all the more because there is no exacting reality behind it to impose a duty or demand a sacrifice. And as Jacobitism survived the Stuarts, so this has outlived the dynasty to which it professes an after-dinner allegiance. It nails a horseshoe over the door, but keeps a rattle by its bedside to summon a more substantial watchman; it hangs a crape on the bee-hives to get a taste of ideal sweetness, but obeys the teaching of the latest bee-book for material and marketable honey. This is the aesthetic variety of the malady, or rather, perhaps, it is only the old complaint robbed of all its pain, and lapped in waking dreams by the narcotism of an age of science. To the world at large it is not undelightful to see the poetical instincts of friends and neighbors finding some other vent than that of verse. But there has been a superstition of very different fibre, of more intense and practical validity, the deformed child of faith, peopling the midnight of the mind with fearful shapes and phrenetic suggestions, a monstrous brood of its own begetting, and making even good men ferocious in imagined self-defence.

Nor is this the only passage in Lowell's essay to which Whittier might have been expected to cry bravo. Lowell never showed his common sense better than when he wrote:

Grimm tells us that he does not know when broomsticks, spits, and similar utensils were first assumed to be the canonical instruments of . . . nocturnal equitation. He thinks it comparatively modern, but I suspect it is as old as the first child that ever bestrode his father's staff, and fancied it into a courser shod with wind, like those of Pindar.

Another comment lies so close to Whittier's own thinking that it might well have been written by the Quaker poet himself, and there is none better worth pondering by his descendants in this age when what used to be regarded as religious wars are viewed with superior horror while ideological conflicts on the secular level are still considered such a sacred duty that we must cross the seven seas to search them out:

If any lesson may be drawn from the tragical and too often disgustful history of witchcraft, it is not one of exultation at our superior enlightenment or shame at the shortcomings of the human intellect. It is rather one of charity and self-distrust. When we see what inhuman absurdities men in other respects wise and good have clung to as the corner-stone of their faith in immortality and a divine ordering of the world, may we not suspect that those who now maintain political or other doctrines which seem to us barbarous and unenlightened may be, for all that, in the main as virtuous and clear-sighted as ourselves?

To all intents and purposes, Whittier's text is reprinted in the following pages as it appeared in the 1847 edition. I have only made a few changes in punctuation and corrected a few obvious errors.

Like many nineteenth-century writers, Whittier often used a dash in combination with another mark of punctuation, generally a comma. We today do not do this, and in these cases I have generally removed one mark or the other. Elsewhere I have modified punctuation only in a few cases, where I felt that what stands in the 1847 edition might be confusing or might slow the reader down; I have not tried to standardize.

The errors I have corrected are very few, and I give a few examples only to indicate their character. I have contributed the umlauts to Freischütz, Erlkönig, and Bürger. When Whittier spells Reginald Scott's name both "Scott" and "Scot" (the *Dictionary of National Biography* gives both spellings), I have thought it just as well to cause him to settle upon one. I have changed one "Wm. Penn" to "William Penn," and, in one case, in the appendix, where Whittier repeats a quotation, using two different forms, neither of them in accord with modern usage, I have standardized. It would seem to me pedantic to footnote such changes, and I have not done so.

Whittier was never known for the accuracy of his quotations (apparently he often quoted from memory, and he once said that he never pretended to quote accurately), and I have simply taken this failing for granted and have not, generally speaking, pointed out his errors. This seemed the more unnecessary since we do not, in all cases, know from what particular text he was quoting.

When it comes to annotation, I am open to censure. There could be only two completely logical ways of treating this text—or any text—(1) to explain *all* allusions, as if one were annotating a freshman reader, or (2) to omit annotation altogether. Believing as I do that one may have too much even of logic, I have done neither. In view of the audience to which this book is addressed, the choice of the first course would have been absurd, and I have not chosen the second because I thought there were points where the reader might wish to have some guidance. I have, therefore, simply tried to explain the more obscure references, wherever, that is, I found it possible to do so. Since not all my readers will be equally erudite, some must inevitably feel that *this* note is quite unnecessary while others will be quite as sure that *that* one ought not to have been left out. But since I have never claimed omniscience, I do not know what I can do except plead guilty on this score and go my way, not too impenitent nor yet greatly bowed down.

Grateful thanks for assistance in annotation are offered to Mr. Roland H. Woodwell, of Amesbury, Massachusetts, Professor John B. Pickard, of the University of Florida, Professor Richard M. Dorson of Indiana University, and the Social Sciences and General Reference departments of the Boston Public Library.

EDWARD WAGENKNECHT

THE SUPERNATURALISM
OF NEW ENGLAND

John Greenleaf Whittier

DEDICATION

DEAR SISTER!—while the wise and sage
Turn coldly from my playful page,
And count it strange that ripened age
   Should stoop to boyhood's folly;
I know that thou wilt judge aright,
Of all which makes the heart more light,
Or lends one star-gleam in the night
   Of clouded Melancholy.

Away with weary cares and themes!—
Swing wide the moon-lit gate of dreams!
Leave free once more the land which teems
   With wonders and romances!
Where thou with clear-discerning eyes,
Shalt rightly read the truth which lies
Beneath the quaintly masking guise
   Of wild and wizard fancies.

Lo! once again our feet we set
On still green wood-paths, twilight wet,
By lonely brooks, whose waters fret

The roots of spectral beeches;
Again the hearth-fire glimmers o'er
Home's white-washed wall and painted floor,
And young eyes widening to the lore
    Of faery folks and witches.

Dear heart!—the legend is not vain
Which lights that holy hearth again,
And, calling back from care and pain,
    And Death's funereal sadness,
Draws round its old familiar blaze,
The clustering groups of happier days,
And lends to sober manhood's gaze
    A glimpse of childish gladness.

And knowing how my life hath been
A weary work of tongue and pen,
A long, harsh strife, with strong-willed men,
    Thou wilt not chide my turning,
To con, at times, an idle rhyme,
To pluck a flower from childhood's clime,
Or listen at Life's noon-day chime
    For the sweet bells of Morning!

INTRODUCTION

A SMALL PORTION of the following pages was published in another form, two or three years ago. I have since been induced to enlarge my magazine paper into a volume embracing the present superstitions and still current traditions of New England, in the hope that, while it will not be found to lack immediate interest, it may hereafter furnish materials for the essayist and poet, who shall one day do for our native land what Scott and Hogg and Burns and Wilson have done for theirs.

The fact that Superstition in one form or another has still such a hold on the common mind, should teach us charity for those who were victims of its grosser errors in past time. We are too prone to forget our own follies, while pondering over those of the generations which have preceded us. The Christians of Spain united in testifying their abhorrence of Mahometan intolerance and conversion by the sword, while engaged themselves in hunting through the passes of the Alpuxarres and along the banks of the Xenil, their feeble and unoffending Moorish and Jewish neighbors. The terrible inquisitors of Goa and Madrid hung the walls of their torture chambers with pictures of the cruelties inflicted upon the early confessors of their faith, and wept over the barbarities of heathen persecution. The English remonstrants against the Piedmont massacres, hung, quartered, and disembowelled the priests of the Catholic Church. The Puritans of New England, while yet smarting from the whip of Episcopal persecution, grubbed off the ears, scarred with hot irons, and strangled on the gallows, those of their own neighbors who could not subscribe to their creed, or pay tithes to their ministers. Thus it is that the language of the present in view of the past, is evermore like that of the Pharisees: "If we had been in the days of our fathers we would not have been partakers with them."

And in the midst of self-congratulations upon our age of light and progress, is it not well to consider that they, who a century from this time shall look back upon our records, may possibly find as much to condemn and sorrow over, as we do in scanning the history of our ancestors? Our partial legislation, our imprisonment for debt, our immoral traffics, our unjust social arrangements, our distinctions on account of complexion and birth, the state of too many of our alms-houses and prisons, our attempts to reconcile freedom and servitude, our vast preparations for war, and our deliberate putting to death of the morally insane on the gallows, may yet be regarded in the clearer light of the coming age, as absurd and as inhuman, as contrary to pure reason and Christianity, as we now consider the witchcraft and religious intolerance of our ancestors.

The clear apprehension which I have, from my own childish experience, of the evil of impressing the young mind with beliefs, unwarranted by reason or revelation, tormenting with strange terror the sleep of childhood, and inducing not infrequently a strong and dangerous reaction in after life, must be my excuse for the slightly disguised sarcasm and ridicule which will be detected in these pages. If in some few instances, like Burns in view of the national thistle, I have

> Turned my weeding hook aside,
> And spared the symbol dear,

I have been influenced by the comparatively innocent nature and simple poetic beauty of the traditions in question; yet, not even for the sake of poetry and romance would I confirm in any mind a pernicious credulity, or seek to absolve myself from that stern duty which the true man owes to his generation, to expose error, whenever and wherever he finds it.

27

CHAPTER I

There be no beggars in this country, but witches too
many.

JOSSELYN's Rarities of New England[1]

"Yankee supernaturalism, forsooth!" methinks I hear the
reader say: "What has your peddling New Englander to do
with matters beyond and above the conception of his sharp-
ened five senses? Can he afford to tenant his houses with
ghosts, who never pay rent? Can he sell city lots in dream-
land? In the midst of his steam-boats and rail-cars—the
whirl and buzz of his machinery—the rattle of his 'notions'
—the chaffer of his bargaining,—can he hear the low voice
which speaks from the Invisible? Ever in a hurry—swallow-
ing his food as he does his physic, as if to taste were perdition—driven through the loom of life like the steam-sent
spindles of his factories—plunging from one speculation to
another, as if the fiery foot of the Evil One were fagging at
his nether extremity—what can he know of that deep, dark
lore, that sublimated abstraction of soul, which has enabled
the still, contemplative German to people even this material

[1] John Josselyn wrote *New England Rarities Discovered in Birds,
Beasts, Fishes, Serpents and Plants of that Country* (1672). Cf. the
references to him in Richard M. Dorson, *Jonathan Draws the Long
Bow* (Harvard University Press, 1946).

nineteenth century with the Shadows and Shapes of the World's Childhood? With senses dulled as to everything but the chink of the 'almighty dollar,' and the true stamp of the genuine bank-note, is he not what Dr. Buchanan[2] would call an 'unimpressible subject'? A man whose worship appears mainly to consist in bowing down to the Demon of Thrift, according to the evangel of Dr. Franklin's Almanac—and who has set up the money-changing temples of his faith all over the land, like altars of Baal in Jeroboam's Israel—what has he to do with the deep, silent workings of the inner life—the unsounded depths of that mysterious ocean, upon whose solemn shores the loud footfalls of Time find no echo?"

Nay, reader, this notion of thine we will charitably pass to the account of thy ignorance of the facts in the case. Beneath the outward mask and habitude of the New England character there is a spiritual activity—an under-current of intense, earnest thought—an infinity of Belief—a capacity for Faith in its most transcendental possibilities. This careful observer will heed, amidst the din of practical and superficial Yankeedom, low, deep, questionings of the Future—the utterance of strange hopes and fears, from spirits nervously conscious, amidst the hurry and glare of life's daily presentments, of the solemn and all-rounding shadow of the Eternal and the Infinite. He will discover no infrequent traces of the Old Superstition—that dark theory of the Invisible World, in which our Puritan ancestors had united

[2] Dr. Joseph Rodes Buchanan (1814–99), lecturer and practitioner. Though he did not publish his *Therapeutic Sarcognomy* and *Manual of Psychometry* until 1884 and 1885 respectively, he was known for his bold theorizing and experimentation even before his graduation from the medical school of the University of Louisville in 1842.

the wild extravagance of Indian tradition with the familiar
and common fantasies of their native land, and that gloomy,
indefinite awe of an agency of Evil which their peculiar
interpretations of the Sacred Volume had inspired—a
theory which threw a veil of mystery over the plainest passages of the great laws of the universe—agitating their entire
community with signs and wonders, and dark marvels—
poisoning the fountains of education, and constituting a
part of their religion. He will find that we, too, can

> listen to our own fond thoughts
> Until they seem no more as Fancy's children;
> Yea, put them on a prophet's robe, endow them
> With prophet-voices;

that our "young men can see visions and our old men
dream dreams." What means, for instance, that strange,
vast, unsubstantial fabric, rising suddenly, like the genii-
built palaces of the Arabian Nights, in the heart of Boston?
Consider well that Temple of the Second Advent[3]—its
thronging thousands, with wild, awe-stricken faces turned
towards the East, like Musselmen to their Kebla,[4] in hourly

[3] Probably the Millerite headquarters, later the Howard Athenaeum, where most of the great actors of the nineteenth century
played, and which, much later, fell upon evil days as the headquarters of strip-tease burlesque in Boston. It burned just in time
to avoid being torn down to make room for the new Scollay Square
Government Center. William Miller (1782–1849) began proclaim-
ing the imminence of the Second Coming of Christ in 1831; he not
only predicted it but set dates for it. Whittier had him in mind in his
specific rejection of millennarian belief in "Our Master."

[4] OED gives "Kebla" as an obsolete form of "Kiblah," the point
in the Temple at Mecca toward which Mohammedans turn when
they pray.

31

expectation of the down-rushing of the fiery mystery of the Apocalypse; waiting with trembling eagerness and "not un-pleasing horror" to behold with the eye of flesh the tremen-dous pageant before which the elements shall melt and the heavens flee away—the Baptism of a World in fire! In what age or quarter of the world has the Supernatural in man taken a more decided and definite shape than this? Look at the nightly gatherings of the "Disciples of the Newness"— grey, thought-worn manhood, and young, dreamy beauty, catching inspiration from the Orphic utterances of modern prophecy, and making glad the weary Present with sunny glimpses of a Transcendental Millennium.[5] Look at Mag-netism, with its fearfully suggestive phenomena, enacting daily in our midst marvels which throw far into shadow the simple witchcraft of our ancestors. What are these but present manifestations of the unearthly and the super-human bursting up through the thin crust of conventional and common-place existence?

Nor is this all. There is scarcely a superstition of the past three centuries which has not at this very time more or less hold upon individual minds among us. In the belief that facts illustrative of this will afford some amusement to the reader, I propose to throw together such as occur to my mind, and which find in New England "a local habitation."

It would perhaps be a question worthy of closer observa-tion than I can well make at the present time, how far the superstitions existing in New England have been modified, and if we may so speak, *acclimated*, by commingling with those of the original inhabitants. The Indian peopled Na-

[5] See James Russell Lowell's sarcastic account of the vagaries of the "transcendental movement" at the beginning of his unsym-pathetic essay on Thoreau in *My Study Windows*.

ture with good and evil intelligences. The waterfall, the lake, the mist, the rock, and tree, had each its spirit. Every species of animal in the woods, and of bird in the air, had its spiritual archetype. The Powah was, in almost all cases, a conjuror, employing magical rites and grotesque incantations to drive away disease or avert misfortune; and it is certain that many of his charms and remedies are still practised among us. The Puritans had no doubt whatever of the diabolical power of their Indian neighbors. Literally they held them to be "children of the Devil." Speaking of their Powahs, Winslow says: "Their Panisees are men of great power and wisdom; and to these the Devil appeareth more familiarly than to others."[6] Cotton Mather's speculations on this point are well known. He dwells with much satisfaction on the spectral Indian warriors who besieged the garrison at Gloucester, impervious even to Christian bullets. He talks mysteriously about the "Black Man," which the Indians told of, who sometimes met them in the woods. Salem witchcraft he satisfactorily traces back to the Indian Titiba in Parson Paris's family.

There is a beautiful and touching incident recorded of

[6] Passaconaway, the great chief of the Pennacooks on the Merrimack, was a celebrated conjuror. In "The Burial of Pennacook" I have alluded to the tradition respecting him:

> Nightly down the river going,
> Swifter was the hunter's rowing,
> When he saw that lodge-fire glowing
>   O'er the water still and red:
> And the squaw's dark eye burned brighter,
> And she drew her blanket tighter,
> As with quicker step, and lighter,
>   From that door she fled.

Tales of him the grey squaw told,
When the winter night wind cold
Pierced her blanket's thickest fold,
   And the fire burned low and small,
Till the very child abed
Drew its bear-skin overhead,
Shrinking from the pale lights shed
   On the trembling wall.

All the subtle spirits hiding
Under earth or wave, abiding
In the caverned rock, or riding
   Misty cloud and mountain breeze,—
Every dark intelligence,
Secret soul and influence
Of all things which outward sense
   Hears, or feels, or sees,—

These the Wizard's skill confessed,
At his bidding banned or blessed,
Stormful woke, or lull'd to rest,
   Wind, and cloud, and fire, and flood;
Burned the drift of bolted snow,
Bade through ice fresh lilies blow,
Greenest leaves of summer grow,
   Over winter's wood!

Not untrue that tale of old!—
Now, as then, the Wise and Bold
All the powers of Nature hold
   Subject to their kingly will:
From the wondering crowds ashore,
Treading Life's wild waters o'er,
As upon a marble floor,
   Moves the Strong Man still.

Still, to such, Life's elements
With their sterner laws dispense,

the Indian preacher HIACOOMES,[7] the first convert to Christianity on Martha's Vine-Yard. While addressing, on one occasion, a large assembly of his red brethren, and while asserting the superiority of his new faith over that in which he had been educated, a celebrated Panisee, whose magical power was everywhere dreaded, made his appearance, in horrid costume, and with the paraphernalia of his art hanging about him. After vainly endeavoring, by strange gestures, contortions, and mutterings, to disturb and terrify the preacher, he placed before him a charm, or "medicine," bidding him keep silence, on pain of instant destruction. The superstitious and half-converted auditors drew back in

---

And the chain of consequence
  Broken in their pathway lies:
Time and Change their vassals making,
Flowers from icy pillows waking,
Tresses of the sunrise shaking
  Over midnight skies.

Still, to the earnest soul, the sun
Rests on towered Gibeon,
And the moon of Ajalon
  Lights the battle-grounds of Life;
To his aid the strong reverses,
Hostile powers, and giant forces,
And the high stars, in their courses,
  Mingle in his strife.

The foregoing is Whittier's note. Edward Winslow (1595–1655), Colonial governor and one of the founders of Plymouth Colony, wrote extensively about the New World.

[7] Hiacoomes was born on Martha's Vineyard about 1610 and died there in 1690. Mayhew's first convert, he is considered the first American Indian to have become a Christian. He began preaching to his people in 1653 and made many converts. In 1670 he was ordained pastor of an Indian church on the Vineyard.

the utmost terror, shrieking and begging their preacher
to desist. Hiacoomes never hesitated. With a loud voice he
defied the magician, told him that his arts had no power
over a servant of the true God, and, in proof of it, trampled
the formidable charm under his feet. This bold act was
more convincing to the astonished spectators than all the
previous sermons of their eloquent teacher. From that day
the once formidable Powah became a laughing-stock on
the island.

It has been said, with far more poetry than truth, that

> The last lingering fiction of the brain,
> The Church-yard GHOST, is laid at rest again.

There is a lurking belief in nearly all minds, that there *may*
be some truth in the idea of departed spirits revisiting the
friends and places familiar to them while in this life. I am
not by any means disposed to enter into an argument in
behalf of this belief. It does not, however, lack greater and
better names than mine to its support. For five thousand
years the entire human family have given it credence. It was
a part of the wild faith of the Scandinavian worshippers of
Odin. It gave a mournful beauty to the battle-songs of the
old Erse and Gaelic bards. It shook the stout heart of the
ancient Roman. It blended with all the wild and extravagant religions of the East. How touching is that death-
scene of Cyrus, as told by Xenophon, when the dying
monarch summoned his children about him, entreating
them to love one another, and to remember that their
father's ghost would be ever at their side, to rejoice with
their rejoicing, and sorrow with their sorrow! All nations,
all ages, as Cicero justly affirms, have given credit to this

ghost-doctrine; and this fact alone, Dr. Johnson argues, fully confirms it. The Doctor himself believed in the ghost of Cocklane. Luther saw, talked, and fought with spirits. Swedenborg made them familiar acquaintances. Coleridge, and his friend, the Apostle of the Unknown Tongues, were spectre-seers. Against so much authority shall we urge the apparently common-sense view of the subject, that the apparition of a disembodied spirit to the sensual organs of sight, hearing, and touch, is a solecism in philosophy—a subversion of all known laws of matter and mind? What will that avail with the man who has actually seen a ghost? Fact before philosophy always. If a man is *certain* he has seen the thing, there is an end of the matter. "Seeing," as the old adage has it, "is believing." Disbelief under such circumstances would justly subject him to the charge which pious father Baxter[8] brought against those who doubted in relation to Cotton Mather's witches: "He must be an obstinate Sadducee who questions it."

There are many who find it difficult to dismiss the whole matter with a sneer. They cannot believe, nor can they, at all times, entirely disbelieve. Our whole being is a mystery. Above, below, around us, all is fearful and wonderful. The lights held by prophets and inspired ones fall indeed upon the solemn portals of a Future Life, but of what is beyond they reveal nothing clearly. Imagination recoils overtasked from the presumptuous effort to penetrate the great uncertainty. Of the capacities of the soul when its incarnation

[8] Richard Baxter (1615–91), author of *The Saint's Everlasting Rest* (1650) and *A Call to the Unconverted* (1657). Whittier admired him in spite of his prejudice against Quakers and notoriously poor judgment and honored him with an essay in his *Old Portraits and Modern Sketches* (1850).

37

is ended, we can only vaguely and unprofitably conjecture. The objection, that, whatever in its new sphere may be the condition and powers of the freed spirit, it can never manifest itself to mortal organs, lies with equal force against the scriptural account of angel visitations, and the apparition of Samuel. The angels which John saw in his awful prophet-trance on Patmos, were the spirits of those who had departed from this stage of being.

On this subject Poetry and Romance have contended successfully with Science and Philosophy. Irving's beautiful Essay[9] still finds a response in the hearts of its readers, and few would wish unwritten these lines of Longfellow:[10]

Ere the evening lamps are lighted,
    And like phantoms, grim and tall,
Shadows from the fitful firelight
    Dance upon my parlor wall;

Then the forms of the departed
    Enter at the open door,
The beloved ones, the true-hearted,
    Come to visit me once more.

With a slow and noiseless footstep
    Comes the messenger divine,
Takes the vacant chair beside me,
    Lays her gentle hand in mine.

And she sits and gazes at me
    With those deep and tender eyes,

[9] Probably "St. Mark's Eve," in *Bracebridge Hall*.

[10] "Footsteps of Angels." Whittier quotes it with substantial, though not complete, accuracy, but the quoted stanzas are not all consecutive.

Like the stars, so still and saint-like,
  Looking downward from the skies.

The lamented Otway Curry—the few fragments of whose dreamy and mysterious poetry have given his memory a place in many hearts—has made this idea of spiritual visitation a familiar theme. The following is from his "Armies of the Eve":

Not in the golden morning shall faded forms return,
For languidly and dimly then the lights of memory burn;
But when the stars are keeping their radiant way on high,
And gentle winds are whispering back the music of the sky.

The dim and shadowy armies of our unquiet dreams,
Their footsteps brush the dewy fern and print the shaded streams;
We meet them in the calmness of high and holier climes,
We greet them with the blessed names of old and happier times,
And moving in the star-light above their sleeping dust,
They freshen all the fountain-springs of our undying trust.

CHAPTER II

One of their fables of a churchyard carcass raised and set a strutting.

BISHOP WARBURTON on Prodigies[1]

Modern scepticism and philosophy have not yet eradicated the belief of supernatural visitation from the New England mind. Here and there—oftenest in our still, fixed, valley-sheltered, unvisited nooks and villages—the Rip Van Winkles of a progressive and restless population—may be still found devout believers worthy of the days of the two Mathers. There are those yet living in this very neighborhood who remember, and relate with an awe which half a century has not abated, the story of Ruth Blaye, the GHOST CHILD! Ruth was a young woman of lively temperament and some personal beauty. While engaged as the teacher of a school in the little town of Southampton, N.H. (whose hills roughen the horizon with their snowy outline within view of my window at this very moment), she was invited to spend an evening at the dwelling of one of her young associates. Suddenly, in the midst of unwonted gaiety, the

[1] William Warburton (1698–1779), editor of Shakespeare and literary executor of Pope. The work referred to is *A Critical and Philosophical Enquiry into the Causes of Prodigies, Miracles* . . . (1729).

young schoolmistress uttered a frightful shriek, and was seen gazing with a countenance of intense horror at the open window; and pointing with her rigid, outstretched arm at an object which drew at once the attention of her companions. Upon the sill of the window, those present saw, or thought they saw, a dead infant, which vanished before they could find words to express their surprise. The wretched Ruth was the first to break the silence. "It is *mine*—MINE—MY CHILD!" she shrieked; "*he has come for me!*" She gradually became more tranquil, but no effort availed to draw from her the terrible secret which was evidently connected with the apparition. She was soon after arrested and brought to trial for the crime of child-murder, found guilty, and executed at Portsmouth, N.H. I do not of course vouch for the truth of this story. "I tell the tale as 'twas told me."

Nearly opposite to my place of residence, on the south side of the Merrimack, stands a house which has long had a bad reputation. One of its recent inmates avers most positively that having on one occasion ventured to sleep in the haunted room, she was visited by a child-ghost which passed through the apartment with a most mournful and unbabylike solemnity. Some of my unbelieving readers will doubtless smile at this, and deem it no matter of surprise that a maiden's slumbers should thus be haunted. As the old playwriter hath it:

> She blushed and smiled to think upon her dream
> Of fondling a sweet infant (with a look
> Like one she will not name) upon her virgin knees.

An esteemed friend—a lady of strong mind, not at all troubled with nervous sensibility, though not deficient in ideality—has told me that while living with an aged relative, who was at that time in the enjoyment of her usual health, she was terrified by the appearance of a dead body lying by the side of her relative, who was quietly sleeping in her bed. The old lady died soon after, and my friend avers that the corpse as it lay before her recalled in the most minute particulars her recollection of the apparition. She had seen the same before by the side of the living sleeper.

A respectable and worthy widow lady, in my neighborhood, professes to be clearly convinced that she saw the spectre of her daughter a little time before her death, while she was yet in perfect health. It crossed the room within a few feet of the mother, in broad day-light. She spoke, but no answer was returned; the countenance of the apparition was fixed and sorrowful. The daughter was at that time absent on a visit to a friend.

I could easily mention other cases some of which have occurred in my immediate vicinity, but the above may serve as a sample of all. I can only say that the character of these ghostseers, in most instances, precludes the idea of imposture or intentional exaggeration on their part. They were undoubtedly suffering under that peculiar disease of the organs of vision, or of the imaginative faculty, which is called "Spectral Illusion," of which so much has of late been written, and of which so little is really known. The case of Professor Hitchcock,[2] detailed by himself in *The New Englander*, is one of the most striking on record. He had, day after day, visions of strange landscapes spread out before him—mountain and lake and forest—vast rocks,

[2] Edward Hitchcock, president of Amherst College and distinguished geologist. The article is "Case of Optical Delusion in Sickness," *New Englander*, III (1845), 199–206.

strata upon strata, piled to the clouds—the panorama of a world shattered and upheaved, disclosing the grim secrets of creation, the unshapely and monstrous rudiments of organic being. Equally remarkable is the case of Dr. Abel, of Lempster, N. H., as given by himself in *The Boston Medical Journal*. While totally blind he saw persons enter his apartment, and especially was he troubled with a grey horse which stood, saddled and bridled, champing his bit, by his bed-side. On one occasion he says:

I seemed placed on the southern border of a plain, from which I could see a whole regiment of soldiers coming from the north. As they approached their number increased to thousands. Their dress was so splendid as to dazzle my sight. Their movements were generally quick, often forced and halting and forming into two columns, facing each other and extending in line as far as the eye could reach. They would then break up and march in different directions, often driving each other in large companies. I felt peculiarly gratified in seeing large groups of little boys running and jumping before and after the troops—many of them dressed in a light blue frock with a scarlet sash. These movements continued through the day till near sunset, when the field was cleared until after ten o'clock, when I saw them returning, but they took a westward movement, and soon disappeared. Among the great variety of moving objects which I have seen, their motion has been from right to left, with very few exceptions, as that of marches and countermarches of the soldiers. It was common to see two objects moving in the same direction, while one would move much faster than the other, and pass by.

To the persons who are the subjects of this illusion the

43

phantoms are real enough—all the more so that they are creations of their own—pictures from within projected outward by the force of Imagination—that tyrant of the mind, enslaving the senses which were intended for its guard against error, and making even their apparently natural action the medium of falsehood. Most readers will remember the account which, about a year ago, circulated through all the newspapers of a spectre seen in Warner, N. H., by two men while watching by the bedside of a dying neighbor. A red, unnatural light filled the room; a stranger suddenly stood beside them, and fixed his eyes upon the dying man who writhed and shrunk beneath the ghastly scrutiny. On the disappearance of the spectre, the sick man made an effort to speak, and in broken words confessed that many years before he had aided in the murder of the man whose spectral image had just left them. This statement, if I recollect rightly, was made under oath. It is but proper, however, to mention, that it has been intimated that the *spirit* seen on this occasion was none other than one of Deacon Giles's sprites of the distillery[3]—one of those bottle imps which play as fantastic tricks with those who uncork them, as *Le Diable Boiteux* of the old French novelist did with the student of Salamanca.[4]

Guilt or remorse for injuries inflicted upon those whose forgiveness cannot be known, and whose power of retaliation in their new condition cannot be estimated, is the prolific mother of spectral annoyances. Whomsoever we have injured, however despicable and weak while living, becomes formidable by death. I have noticed in our thrifty, money-loving community, that there is a very common

[3] A local reference.
[4] Alan René Le Sage, *The Devil upon Two Sticks* (1707).

notion that the disposal of an estate contrary to the known wishes of the testator is the most potent spell of all others for raising a Yankee ghost. Among the many anecdotes which corroborate this opinion, I must content myself with citing one, the scene of which happens to be in an adjoining town.

Some years ago, an elderly woman, familiarly known as "Aunt Morse" died, leaving a handsome little property. No will was found, although it was understood before her decease that such a document was in the hands of Squire S., one of her neighbors. One cold winter evening, some weeks after her departure, Squire S. sat in his parlor looking over his papers, when, hearing some one cough in a familiar way, he looked up, and saw before him a little crooked old woman in an oil-nut colored woollen frock, blue and white tow and linen apron, and striped blanket, leaning her sharp pinched face on one hand, while the other supported a short black tobacco-pipe, at which she was puffing in the most vehement and spiteful manner conceivable.

The Squire was a man of some nerve; but his first thought was to attempt an escape, from which he was deterred only by the consideration that any effort to that effect would necessarily bring him nearer to his unwelcome visitor.

"Aunt Morse," he said at length, "for the Lord's sake, get right back to the burying-ground! What on earth are you here for?"

The apparition took her pipe deliberately from her mouth, and informed him that she came to see justice done with her will; and that nobody need think of cheating her, dead or alive. Concluding her remark with a shrill emphasis, she replaced her pipe and puffed away with renewed vigor. The Squire had reasons for retaining the document at issue, which he had supposed conclusive, but he had not reckoned upon the interference of the testator in the matter. Aunt Morse, when living, he had always regarded as a very shrew of a woman; and he now began to suspect that her recent change of condition had improved her, like Sheridan's ghost, "the wrong way." He saw nothing better to be done under the circumstances than to promise to see the matter set right that very evening.

The Ghost nodded her head approvingly, and, knocking the ashes out of her pipe against the chimney, proceeded to fill it anew with a handful of tobacco from her side pocket. "And now, Squire," she said, "if you'll just light my pipe for me, I'll be a going."

The Squire was, as has been intimated, no coward; he had been out during the war in a Merrimack privateer, and had seen sharp work off Fayal, but, as he said afterwards, "it was no touch to lighting Aunt Morse's pipe." No slave of a pipe-bearer ever handed the chibouque to the Grand Turk with more care and reverence, than the Squire manifested on this occasion. Aunt Morse drew two or three long preliminary whiffs, to see that all was right, pulled her blanket over her hand, and slowly hobbled out at the door. The Squire being true to his promise was never again disturbed. It is right to say that there were strong suspicions at the time, that the ghost was a reality of flesh and blood,—in short, one of the living heirs of Aunt Morse, and not the old lady herself.

CHAPTER III

Our mothers' mayds have so frayed us with an ugly
Divil having hornes on his hedde, fire in his mouth,
and a tayle at his back, whereby we starte and are afraid
when we hear one cry, Boh!

REGINALD SCOTT

Warnings of change and disaster—signs and omens of
approaching calamity—are as carefully noted at the present
day in some of our rural districts as they were in ancient
Rome. The superstition seems inwrought and permanent—
a part of the popular mind. I have rarely met with a person
entirely free from its influence. Who has not at times, under
circumstances of deep depression, nervous disarrangement,
or physical illness, or in those peculiar moods of the spirit
when even "the grasshopper is a burden," felt his flesh creep
at the howl of a dog at midnight—the tick of a harmless
insect in the wall—any unusual sight or sound, the cause of
which does not at once suggest itself—things in themselves
trivial and meaningless, calling up dark and dread associa-
tions? There are, I believe, times when the stoutest materialist reveals his deep and abiding awe of the invisible and the
unknown; when, like Eliphaz the Temanite, he feels a
"spirit passing before him, the form of which is not dis-
cerned." For one, I confess there are seasons when I love to
con over Increase Mather's *Remarkable Providences*,[1] or Dr.

[1] *An Essay for the Recording of Illustrious Providences* (1684).

More's[2] *Continuation of Glanville,* or any other chronicle of the marvellous, with which the divines of former days edified the people. I know very well that our modern theologians, as if to atone for the credulity of their order formerly, have unceremoniously turned witchcraft, ghost-seeing, and second sight, into Milton's receptacle of exploded follies and detected impostures:

> Over the backside of the world far off,
> Into a limbo broad and large, and called
> The paradise of fools;

—that indeed out of their peculiar province, and apart from the phenomena of their vocation, they have become the most thorough skeptics and unbelievers among us. Yet, as Falstaff said of his wit, if they have not the marvellous themselves, they are the cause of it in others.[3] In certain states of mind the very sight of a clergyman in his sombre professional garb, is sufficient to awaken all the wonderful within me. My imagination goes wandering back to the subtle priesthood of mysterious Egypt—I think of Jannes and

[2] Probably Henry More (1614–87), who contributed to, and perhaps edited, Joseph Glanvill's *Sadducisimus Triumphatus* (1681) and annotated his *Lux Orientalis* (1682). Glanvill (1636–80) was greatly interested in what would now be called parapsychology or psychical research. Among his works is *Philosophical Considerations Touching Witches and Witchcraft* (1666). The fourth (1668) edition was called *A Blow at Modern Sadducism, in Some Philosophical Considerations about Witchcraft . . . .*

[3] This quotation is badly garbled even for Whittier. What Falstaff said (2 *Henry IV,* Act I, scene 2) is, of course, "I am not only witty in myself, but the cause that wit is in other men."

Jambres[4]—of the Persian Magi—dim oakgroves with Druid altars, and priests and victims rise before me. For what is the priest even of our New England but a living testimony to the truth of the supernatural and the reality of the unseen—a man of mystery, walking in the shadow of the ideal world—by profession an expounder of spiritual wonders? Laugh he may at the old tales of astrology and witchcraft and demoniacal possession, but does he not believe and bear testimony to his faith in the reality of that Dark Essence which Scripture more than hints at—which has modified more or less all the religious systems and speculations of the heathen world—the Ahriman of the Parsee, the Pluto of the Roman mythology, the Devil of the Jew and Christian, the Shitan of the Mussulman, the Machinito of the Indian—evil in the universe of goodness, darkness in the light of Divine intelligence—in itself the great and crowning mystery from which by no unnatural process of imagination may be deduced everything which our forefathers believed of the spiritual world and supernatural agency? That fearful being with his tributaries and agents—"the Devil and his angels"—how awfully he rises before us in the brief outline limning of the sacred writers! How he glooms, "in shape and gesture proudly eminent," on the immortal canvass of Milton and Dante! What a note of horror does his name throw into the sweet Sabbath psalmody of our churches? What strange, dark fancies are connected with the very language of our common law indictments, when our grand juries find under oath that the offence com-

---

[4] So Saint Paul (2 Timothy 3:8) denominates the Egyptian magicians who contended against Moses (Exodus, chs. 5ff.).

plained of has been committed "at the instigation of the devil"!

How hardly effaced are the impressions of childhood! Even at this day, at the mention of the Evil Angel, an image rises before me, like that with which I used especially to horrify myself in an old copy of *Pilgrim's Progress*. Horned, hoofed, scaly and fire-breathing, his caudal extremity twisted tight with rage, I remember him, illustrating the tremendous encounter of Christian in the valley where "Apollyon straddled over the whole breadth of the way." There was another print of the enemy, which made no slight impression upon me; it was the frontispiece of an old, smoked, snuff-stained pamphlet, the property of an elderly lady (who had a fine collection of similar wonders wherewith she was kind enough to edify her young visitors), containing a solemn account of the fate of a wicked dancing party in New Jersey, whose irreverent declaration that they would have a fiddler if they had to send to the lower regions for him, called up the fiend himself, who forthwith commenced playing, while the company danced to the music incessantly, without the power to suspend their exercise until their feet and legs were worn off to the knees! The rude wood-cut represented the Demon Fiddler and his agonized companions literally *stumping* it up and down in "cotillions, jigs, strathspeys and reels." He would have answered very well to the description of the infernal piper in Tam O'Shanter:

> A winnock-bunker in the east
> There sat Auld Nick in shape o' beast,
> A towzie tyke, black, grim and large,
> To gie them music was his charge.

To this popular notion of the impersonation of the principle of evil, we are doubtless indebted for the whole dark legacy of witchcraft, possession, demons, &c. Failing in their efforts to solve the dark problem of the origin of evil, men fall back upon the idea of a malignant being—the antagonism of good. Of this mysterious and dreadful personification, we find ourselves constrained to speak with a degree of that awe and reverence which are always associated with undefined power and the ability to harm. "The devil," says an old writer, "is a dignity, although his glory be somewhat faded and wan, and is to be spoken of accordingly." Cudworth,[5] in his Intellectual System, says that "the inferior gods or demons being all of them able to do us hurt or good, and being also irascible, and therefore provocable by our neglect, it is our interest to appease and pacify them."

Henry of Nettesheim[6] says, "That it is unanimously maintained that devils do wander up and down in the earth, but what they are, or how they are, ecclesiasticals have not clearly expounded." Origen, from whose speculations on this subject the author of *Festus*[7] seems to have derived the plan of his poem, thought them to be spirits who, by repentance, might be restored, that in the end all knees should be bowed to the Father of Spirits, and He become all in all.

[5] Ralph Cudworth (1617–88), English philosopher and Cambridge don, author of *True Intellectual System of the Universe* (1678).

[6] Heinrich Cornelius Agrippa von Nettesheim (1486–1535), German philosopher and alchemist, author of *De Occulta Philosophia* (1510). He is referred to elsewhere as Cornelius Agrippa and Henry Cornelius Agrippa.

[7] *Festus* (1839, 1845), a version of the Faust story, by Philip James Bailey (1816–1902), English poet.

Justin Martyr was of the opinion that many of them still hoped for their salvation, and the Cabalists held that this hope of theirs was well founded. One is irresistibly reminded here of the closing verse of the "Address to the Deil," by Burns:

But fare ye weel, Auld Nickie ben!
Gin ye wad take a thought and mend
Ye aiblins might,—I dinna ken—
    Still hae a stake:
I'm wae to think upon your den
    E'en for your sake.

The charity of the poet certainly has one characteristic of the Christian virtue of that name; it "covers a multitude of sins."

The old schoolmen and fathers seem to agree that the Devil and his ministers have bodies in some sort material, subject to passions, and liable to injury and pain. Origen has a curious notion that any evil spirit who, in a contest with a human being, is defeated, loses from thenceforth all power of mischief, and may be compared to a wasp who has lost his sting.

Our Puritan writers seem to have pursued their investigations of Demonology with a zeal and perseverance scarcely to be conceived of at the present day. I shall take occasion in another place to refer to their labors. I do not recollect of ever meeting with but one sane person who believed he had seen the Arch-adversary. He is a man of strong nerves, sound judgment in ordinary matters, and not particularly superstitious. He states that several years ago, when his mind was somewhat "exercised," to use his own words, on the subject of his religious duties, he was standing one moonlight evening, in a meditative mood, on the bridge which crosses Little River near its junction with the Merrimack. Suddenly he became sensible of a strange feeling, as if something terrible was near at hand; a vague terror crept over him. "I *knew*," said he, in relating the story, "that something bad and frightful was behind me—I *felt* it. And when I did look round, there on the bridge, within a few paces of me, a huge black dog was sitting, with the face of a man—a human face, if ever I saw one, turned full up to the moonlight. It remained just long enough to give me a clear view of it, and then vanished; and ever since, when I think of Satan, I call to mind the Dogman on the bridge."

"The Devil," said Samson Occum,[8] the famous Indian preacher, in a discourse on Temperance, "is a gentleman, and never drinks." Nevertheless, it is a remarkable fact, and worthy of the serious consideration of all who "tarry long at the wine," that, in that state of the drunkard's malady known as *delirium tremens*, the adversary, in some shape or other, is generally visible to the sufferers, or, at least, as Winslow says of the Powahs, "he appeareth more familiarly to them than to others." I recollect a statement made to me by a gentleman who has had bitter experience of the evils of intemperance, and who is at this time devoting his fine talents to the cause of philanthropy and mercy, as the editor of one of our best Temperance Journals, which left a most vivid impression on my mind. He had just returned from a sea-voyage; and, for the sake of enjoying a debauch unmolested by his friends, took up his abode in a rum-selling tavern in a somewhat lonely location on the sea-board. Here he drank for many days without stint, keeping himself the

---

[8] Samson Occum (1723–92), American Indian preacher. Both *DAB* and *Century Dictionary of Names* spell his name "Occom."

whole time in a state of semi-intoxication. One night he stood leaning against a tree, looking listlessly and vacantly out upon the ocean; the waves breaking on the beach, and the white sails of passing vessels, vaguely impressing him like the pictures of a dream. He was startled by a voice whispering hoarsely in his ear: *You have mur-der-ed a man; the of-fi-cers of jus-tice are af-ter you: you must fly for your life!"* Every syllable was pronounced slowly and separately, and there was something in the hoarse, gasping sound of the whisper which was indescribably dreadful. He looked around him, and seeing nothing but the clear moonlight on the grass, became partially sensible that he was the victim of illusion, and a sudden fear of insanity thrilled him with a momentary terror. Rallying himself, he returned to the tavern, drank another glass of brandy, and retired to his chamber. He had scarcely lain his head on the pillow when he heard that hoarse, low, but terribly distinct whisper, repeating the same words. He describes his sensations at this time as inconceivably fearful. Reason was struggling with insanity, but amidst the confusion and mad disorder, one terrible thought evolved itself. Had he *not*, in a moment of phrensy, of which his memory made no record, actually murdered some one? And was not this a warning from Heaven? Leaving his bed, and opening the door, he heard the words again repeated, with the addition, in a tone of intense earnestness, "Follow me." He walked forward in the direction of the sound, through a long entry to the head of a staircase, where he paused for a moment, when again he heard the whisper, half way down the stairs: "Follow me!"

Trembling with terror, he passed down two flights of stairs, and found himself treading on the cold brick floor of a large room in the basement or cellar, where he had never been before. The voice still beckoned him onward. Groping after it, his hand touched an upright post, against which he leaned for a moment. The voice again spoke, apparently only two or three yards in front of him: "You *have* mur-der-ed a man!—the of-fi-cers are close behind you! Follow me!" Putting one foot forward while his hand still grasped the post, it fell upon empty air, and he with difficulty recovered himself. Stooping down, and feeling with his hands, he found himself on the very edge of a large uncovered cistern or tank, filled well nigh to the top with water! The sudden shock of this discovery broke the horrible enchantment. The whisperer was silent. He believed at the time that he had been the subject and well nigh the victim of a diabolical delusion; and he states that, even now, with the recollection of that strange whisper is always associated a thought of the universal Tempter.

CHAPTER IV

Still o'er life's woe and penury
    Let graceful tendrils twine,
And o'er its hard and rugged ways,
    Hang Fancy's green ensign.
The stateliest tree, around whose base
    No wreathing vine has grown;
Stands harshly, with its rough bare roots
    From the shrunk earth upthrown!

The practice of charms, or what is popularly called "trying projects," is still, to some extent, continued among us. The inimitable description which Burns gives of similar practices in his Halloween may not in all respects apply to our domestic conjurations, but the following needs only the substitution of apple-seeds for nuts:

The auld gude wife's weel-hoordet nits
    Are round an' round divided,
An' mony lads and lassies fates
    Are there that night decided:
Some kindle couthie side by side

An' burn thegither trimly,
Some start awa wi' saucy pride,
An' jump out owre the chimilie.

One of the most perilous of these "projects" is as follows: A young woman goes down into the cellar, or into a dark room, with a mirror in her hand, and looking into it sees the face of her future husband peering at her through the darkness—the mirror being, for the time, as potent as the famous Cambuscan glass of which Chaucer discourses. A neighbor of mine, in speaking on this conjuration, insists that there is something in it, and adduces a case in point. One of her school-mates made the experiment, and saw the face of a strange man in the glass; and many years afterwards she saw the very man pass her father's door. He proved to be an English emigrant, just landed, and in due time became her husband. Burns alludes to something like the spell above described.

Wee Jenny to her Grannie says,
"Will ye go wi' me, Grannie?
To eat an apple at the glass,
I got from uncle Johnnie."
She fuff't her pipe wi sic a lunt,
In wrath she was so vaporin,
She noticed na an 'azle brunt
Her bran new worset apron.

"Ye little skelpan-limmer's face,
How dare ye try sic sportin,
An' seek the foul thief ony place,
For him to try your fortune?—

Nae doubt but ye may get a *sight!*
Great cause ye hae to fear it;

57

For mony a one has gotten a fright,
An' lived and died deleerit."

It is not to be denied that this amusing and sportive
juvenile glammary[1] has seen its best days in New England.
We are getting too practical, worldly, and sensible withal
for it. The schoolmaster has been abroad to some purpose.
Not without results have our Lyceum Lecturers, and
Travels of Peter Parley, brought everything in Heaven
above and in the earth below to the level of childhood's
capacities. It has been well said, by a recent writer, that
children of the present day are ashamed to act like children.
That it was ever otherwise, is getting to be a matter of tradition, scarcely to be credited. In our cities and large towns,
children nowadays pass through the opening acts of life's
marvellous drama with as little manifestation of wonder
and surprise, as the Indian does through the streets of a
civilized city, which he has entered for the first time. Yet
nature, sooner or later, vindicates her mysteries; voices from
the unseen penetrate the din of civilisation. The child-
philosopher and materialist often becomes the visionary of
riper years, running into illuminism, magnetism, and trans-
cendentalism with its inspired priests and priestesses, its
Revelations and oracular responses.

But in many a green valley of rural New England, there
are children yet: boys and girls are still to be found, not
quite overtaken by the march of mind. There too are Huskings and Apple-bees, and Quilting-parties; and huge old-
fashioned fire-places, piled with crackling walnut, flinging
its rosy light over happy countenances of youth and scarcely

[1] OED gives "glammerie" as an obsolete form of "glamoury,"
meaning glamour or magic.

58

less happy age. If it be true that, according to Cornelius Agrippa, "A wood fire doth drive away dark spirits," it is nevertheless also true that around it the simple superstitions of our ancestors still love to linger; and there the half-sportful, half-serious charms and auguries of which I have spoken are oftenest resorted to. It would be altogether out of place to think of them by our black and unsightly stoves, or the dull and dark monotony of our furnace-heated rooms. Within the circle of the light of the open fire, safely might the young conjurors question Destiny, for none but kindly and gentle messengers from Wonderland could venture among them. And, who of us, looking back to those long autumnal evenings of childhood, when the glow of the kitchen-fire rested on the beloved faces of Home, does not feel that there is truth and beauty in what the quaint old author just quoted affirms? "As the spirits of darkness grow stronger in the dark, so good spirits which are angels of light are multiplied and strengthened not only by the divine light of the sun and stars, but also by the light of our common wood-fires."

Fairy-faith is, we may safely say, now dead everywhere—buried, indeed, for the mad painter, Blake,[2] saw the funeral of the last of the little people, and an irreverent English Bishop has sung their requiem. It never had much hold upon the Yankee mind—our superstitions being mostly of a grimmer, and less poetical kind. The Irish Presbyterians, who settled in New Hampshire about the year 1720, brought, indeed, with them, among other strange matters,

[2] In a letter of 1864, Whittier wrote of Blake: "The man was a marvel—perhaps a great deal more sane than most of us—ever reaching out from the shows and shadows of time and sense to the things unseen 'by the outward eye' which are eternal."

potatoes and fairies, but while the former took root and flourished among us, the latter died out, after lingering a few years, in a very melancholy and disconsolate way, doubtlessly looking regretfully back to their green turf dances, moonlight revels, and cheerful nestling around the shealing-fires of Ireland. The last that has been heard of them, was some forty or fifty years ago, in a tavern-house in S———, N. H. The landlord was a spiteful little man, whose sour, pinched look was a standing libel upon the state of his larder. He made his house so uncomfortable by his moroseness that travellers even at nightfall pushed by his door, and drove to the next town. Teamsters and drovers, who, in those days, were apt to be very thirsty, learned, even before temperance societies were thought of, to practise total abstinence on that road, and cracked their whips, and goaded on their teams, in full view of a most tempting array of bottles and glasses, from behind which the surly little landlord glared out upon them, with a look which seemed expressive of all sorts of evil wishes, broken legs, overturned carriages, spavined horses, sprained oxen, unsavory poultry, damaged butter, and bad markets. And if, as a matter of necessity, to "keep the cold out of his stomach," occasionally a wayfarer stopped his team, and ventured to call for "somethin' warmin,'" the testy publican stirred up the beverage in such a spiteful way, that, on receiving it foaming from his hand, the poor customer was half afraid to open his mouth, lest the red-hot flip-iron should be plunged down his gullet.

As a matter of course, poverty came upon the house and its tenants like an armed man. Loose clap-boards rattled in the wind; rags fluttered from the broken windows; within doors were tattered children and scanty fare. The landlord's wife was a stout, buxom woman, of Irish lineage, and what with scolding her husband and liberally patronizing his bar in his absence, managed to keep, as she said, her "own heart whole," although the same could scarcely be said of her children's trousers and her own frock of homespun. She confidently predicted that "a betther day was coming," being, in fact, the only thing hopeful about the premises. And it did come sure enough. Not only all the regular travellers on the road made a point of stopping at the tavern, but guests from all the adjacent towns filled its long-deserted rooms. The secret of which was, that it had somehow got abroad that a company of fairies had taken up their abode in the hostelry, and daily held conversation with each other in the capacious parlor. I have heard those who at the time visited the tavern say that it was literally thronged for several weeks. Small, squeaking voices, spoke in a sort of Yankee-Irish dialect, in the haunted room, to the astonishment and admiration of hundreds. The inn, of course, was blessed by this fairy visitation; the clap-boards ceased their racket, clear panes took the place of rags in the sashes, and the little till under the bar grew daily heavy with coin. The magical influence extended even farther; for it was observable that the landlord wore a good-natured face, and that the landlady's visits to the gin-bottle were less and less frequent. But the thing could not, in the nature of the case, continue long. It was too late in the day, and on the wrong side of the water. As the novelty wore off, people began to doubt and reason about it. Had the place been traversed by a ghost, or disturbed by a witch, they could have acquiesced in it very quietly, but this outlandish belief in fairies was altogether an overtask for Yankee credulity. As might have been expected, the little strangers, unable to breathe in an atmosphere of doubt and suspicion, soon took their leave, shaking off the dust of their elfin feet, as a testimony against an unbelieving generation. It was indeed said, that certain rude fellows from the Bay State pulled away a board from the ceiling, and disclosed to view the fairies in the shape of the landlady's three slatternly daughters. But, the reader who has any degree of that "charity which thinketh no evil," will rather credit the statement of the fairies themselves, as reported by the mistress of the house; "that they were tired of the new country, and had no pace of their lives among the Yankees, and were going back to ould Ireland."

It is a curious fact that the Indians had some notion of a race of beings corresponding in many respects to the English fairies. Schoolcraft describes them as small creatures in human shape, inhabiting rocks, crags, and romantic dells, and delighting especially in points of land jutting into lakes and rivers, and which were covered with pine trees. They were called Puckweedjinees, little vanishers.

It is to be regretted that our Puritan ancestors did not think it worth their while to hand down to us more of the simple and beautiful traditions and beliefs of the "heathen round about" them. Some hints of them we glean from the writings of the missionary Mayhew,[3] and the curious little book of Roger Williams.[4] Especially would one like to know more of that domestic demon, Wetuomanit, who presided

[3] The younger Thomas Mayhew (c. 1621–57) began missionary work among the Indians on Martha's Vineyard, which was carried on after his death by his father, Thomas Mayhew (1593–1682), and later by Experience Mayhew (1673–1758), grandson of the younger Thomas.

[4] Probably A Key to the Languages of America (1643).

over household affairs, assisted the young squaw in her first essay at wigwam keeping, gave timely note of danger, and kept evil spirits at a distance—a kind of New World Brownie, gentle and useful, a belief in whom does not really appear to us, as it did to the painful old Fathers of New England orthodoxy, "nefarious and very devilish."

Very beautiful, too, is the story of Pumooolah—a mighty spirit, whose home is on the great Katahdin mountain, sitting there, with his earthly bride (a beautiful daughter of the Penobscots, transformed into an immortal by her love), in serenest sunshine, above the storm which crouches and growls at his feet. None but the perfectly pure and good can reach his abode. Many have from time to time attempted it in vain; some, after almost reaching the summit, have been driven back by thunderbolts or sleety whirlwinds.

Brainard, who truly deserves the name of an American poet, has left behind him a ballad on the Indian legend of the Black Fox, which haunted Salmon River, a tributary of the Connecticut. Its wild and picturesque beauty causes us to regret that more of the still lingering traditions of the Red Men have not been made the themes of his verse:—

The Black Fox

How cold, how beautiful, how bright
  The cloudless heaven above us shines!
But 'tis a howling winter's night—
  'Twould freeze the very forest pines!

The winds are up while mortals sleep;
  The stars look forth while eyes are shut;
The bolted-snow lies drifted deep
  Around our poor and lonely hut.

63

With silent step and listening ear,
　With bow and arrow, dog and gun,
We'll mark his track—his prowl we hear—
　Now is our time!—Come on, come on!

O'er many a fence, through many a wood,
　Following the dog's bewildered scent,
In anxious haste and earnest mood,
　The white man and the Indian went.

The gun is cocked, the bow is bent,
　The dog stands with uplifted paw;
And ball and arrow both are sent,
　Aimed at the prowler's very jaw.

The ball to kill that Fox is run,
　Not in a mould by mortals made;
The arrow which that Fox should shun
　Was never shaped from earthly reed!

The Indian Druids of the wood
　Know where the fatal arrows grow;
They spring not by the summer flood,
　They pierce not through the winter's snow!

Why cowers the dog, whose snuffing nose
　Was never once deceived till now?
And why amidst the chilling snows
　Does either hunter wipe his brow?

For once they see his fearful den;
　'Tis a dark cloud that slowly moves
By night around the homes of men,
　By day along the stream it loves.

Again the dog is on the track,
   The hunters chase o'er dale and hill;
They may not, though they would, look back,
   They must go forward, forward still.

Onward they go, and never turn,
   Amidst a night which knows no day;
For never more shall morning sun
   Light them upon their endless way.

The hut is desolate; and there
   The famished dog alone returns;
On the cold steps he makes his lair;
   By the shut door he lays his bones.

Now the tired sportsman leans his gun
   Against the ruins on its site,
And ponders on the hunting done
   By the lost wanderers of the night.

And there the little country girls
   Will stop to whisper, listen and look,
And tell, while dressing their sunny curls,
   Of the Black Fox of Salmon Brook!

CHAPTER V

    Tamar.—But are they round us, Hadad? Not confined
In penal chains and darkness?
    Hadad.   So he said,
And so your sacred books infer. What saith
Your prophet?—What the prince of Uz?
    Tamar.   I shudder
Lest some dark minister be near us now!

                                       —Hadad[1]

Elderly people in this region yet tell marvellous stories
of General M., of Hampton, N. H.,[2] especially of his league
with the Devil, who used to visit him occasionally in the
shape of a small man in a leathern dress. The general's house
was once burned, in revenge, as it is said, by the fiend, whom
the former had outwitted. He had agreed, it seems, to
furnish the general with a boot-full of gold and silver poured
annually down the chimney. The shrewd Yankee cut off, on
one occasion, the foot of the boot, and the Devil kept pouring down the coin from the chimney's top, in a vain attempt to fill it, until the room was literally filled with the
precious metal. When the general died, he was laid out,
and put in a coffin as usual; but, on the day of the funeral,
it was whispered about that his body was missing; and the
neighbors came to the charitable conclusion that the enemy
had got his own at last.

[1] Poetic drama (1825) by James Abraham Hillhouse (1789–
1841), of New Haven.

[2] Theodore Roosevelt Garrison points out that General M has

The following Ballad is founded upon one of the marvellous legends connected with this Yankee Faust. I remember hearing the story, when a child, from a venerable family visitant.

The New Wife and the Old

Dark the halls, and cold the feast—
Gone the bridesmaids, gone the Priest!
All is over—all is done,
Twain of yesterday are one!
Blooming girl and manhood grey,
Autumn in the arms of May!

Hushed within and hushed without,
Dancing feet and wrestlers' shout;
Dies the bonfire on the hill;
All is dark and all is still,
Save the starlight, save the breeze
Moaning through the grave-yard trees;
And the great sea-waves below,
Pulse o' the midnight, beating slow.

From the brief dream of a bride
She hath wakened, at his side.
With a half uttered shriek and start—
Feels she not his beating heart?
And the pressure of his arm,
And his breathing, near and warm?

Lightly from the bridal bed
Springs that fair dischevelled head,

been identified by Samuel G. Drake as General Jonathan Moulton; see
the latter's *Annals of Witchcraft in the United States* (1869).

And a feeling, new, intense,
Half of shame, half innocence,
Maiden fear and wonder, speaks
Through her lips and changing cheeks.

From the oaken mantel glowing
Faintest light the lamp is throwing
On the mirror's antique mould,
High-backed chair, and wainscot old,
And, through faded curtains stealing,
His dark sleeping face revealing.

Listless lies the strong man there,
Silver-streaked his careless hair;
Lips of love have left no trace
On that hard and haughty face;
And that forehead's knitted thought
Love's soft hand hath not unwrought.

"Yet," she sighs, "he loves me well,
More than these calm lips will tell.
Stooping to my lowly state,
He hath made me rich and great,
And I bless him, though he be
Hard and stern to all save me!"

While she speaketh falls the light
O'er her fingers small and white;
Gold and gem, and costly ring
Back the timid lustre fling—
Love's selectest gifts and rare,
His proud hand hath fastened there.

Gratefully she marks the glow
From those tapering lines of snow;

Fondly o'er the sleeper bending
His black hair with golden blending,
In her soft and light caress,
Cheek and lip together press.

Ha!—that start of horror!—Why
That wild stare and wilder cry,
Full of terror, full of pain?
Is there madness in her brain?
Hark! that gasping hoarse and low:
"Spare me—spare me—let me go!"

God have mercy!—Icy cold
Spectral hands her own enfold,
Drawing silently from them
Love's fair gifts of gold and gem,
"Waken! save me!" still as death
At her side he slumbereth.

Ring and bracelet all are gone,
And that ice-cold hand withdrawn;
But she hears a murmur low,
Full of sweetness, full of woe,
Half a sigh and half a moan:
"Fear not! Give the dead her own!"

Ah!—the dead wife's voice she knows!
That cold hand whose pressure froze,
Once in warmest life had borne
Gem and band her own hath worn.
"Wake thee! Wake thee!" Lo, his eyes
Open with a dull surprise.

In his arms the strong man folds her,
Closer to his breast he holds her;

Trembling limbs his own are meeting,
And he feels her heart's quick beating;
"Nay, my dearest, why this fear?"
"Hush!" she saith, "the dead is here!"

"Nay, a dream—an idle dream."
But before the lamp's pale gleam
Tremblingly her hand she raises,—
There no more the diamond blazes,
Clasp of pearl or ring of gold,—
"Ah!" she sighs, "her hand was cold!"

Broken words of cheer he saith,
But his dark lip quivereth,
And as o'er the Past he thinketh,
From his young wife's arms he shrinketh;
Can those soft arms round him lie,
Underneath his dead wife's eye?

She her fair young head can rest
Soothed and child-like on his breast,
And in trustful innocence
Draw new strength and courage thence;
He, the proud man, feels within
But the cowardice of Sin!

She can murmur in her thought
Simple prayers her mother taught,
And His blessed angels call,
Whose great love is over all;
He, alone, in prayerless pride,
Meets the dark Past at her side!

One, who living shrank with dread,
From his look or word or tread,

Unto whom her early grave
Was as freedom to the slave,
Moves him at this midnight hour,
With the dead's unconscious power!

Ah, the dead, the unforgot!
From their solemn homes of thought,
Where the cypress shadows blend
Darkly over foe and friend,
Or in love or sad rebuke,
Back upon the living look.

And the tenderest ones and weakest,
Who their wrongs have borne the meekest,
Lifting from those dark still places,
Sweet and sad remembered faces,
O'er the guilty hearts behind
An unwitting triumph find.

Haunted houses are becoming scarce in New England. Formerly every village could boast one or more of these favored tenements. I have, nevertheless, seen several of a most unchristian reputation in this respect,—old, black, and unseemly, with shingles and clap-boards hanging loose and ragged, like the cloak of Otway's witch.[3] A new coat of paint, in almost all cases, proves an effectual exorcism. A former neighbor of mine—a simple, honest mechanic—used to amuse us by his reiterated complaints of the diabolical revels of certain evil spirits, which had chosen his garret for their ball-room. All night long he could hear a dance going

[3] Thomas Otway (1652–85), in his play, *The Orphan* (1680). Whittier quotes the description in "New England Superstitions," which is reprinted in Appendix A to this volume.

71

on above him, regulated by some infernal melody. He had no doubt whatever of the supernatural character of the annoyance, and treated with contempt the suggestion of his neighbors, that, after all, it might be nothing more than the rats among his corn.

Any one who has read Increase Mather's *Remarkable Providences*, or the second volume of *Magnalia*, p. 391–2, will remember the story of the house in Newbury, on the Merrimack, which was "infested by demons," and where, "before the Devil was chained up, the invisible hand did begin to put forth an astonishing visibility." This house is still standing at the corner of Market street and opposite St. Paul's Church, in the pleasant town of Newburyport—a venerable and respectable mansion, half hidden by aged trees. Here, in 1679, lived a sober old couple, William Morse and his wife Elizabeth, and their grandson, a roguish lad of fifteen, who seems to have been the author of the mischief. The whole neighborhood was filled with consternation by accounts of strange disturbances in this dwelling: doors opening and shutting; pots and kettles dancing on the floor; the dinner-pot, after being hung over the fire carefully by the good wife, persisting in turning itself over, and emptying the pork and cabbage in the fire; the bed-clothes flying off as fast as they could be put on; and the great wooden wheel turning itself upside down, and standing on its end, in a manner very unseemly and improper for a piece of Puritan housing-stuff. A sea-faring man, named Powell, detected the young mischief-maker, and put an end to the disturbance; but, for so doing, he was himself suspected of being a wizard, was arrested and tried at Salem, and narrowly escaped the gallows. On his acquittal, the good citizens seized upon Morse's wife as the witch, and she was actually sentenced to be executed, but was finally reprieved by the Governor and Council. A full and accurate account of this case may be found in Coffin's quaint History of Newbury, pp. 122–34.

About two miles from my residence are the ruins of a mill, in a narrow ravine fringed with trees. Some forty years ago the mill was supposed to be haunted, and horse-shoes, in consequence, were nailed over its doors. One worthy man, whose business lay beyond the mill, was afraid to pass it alone, and his wife, who was less fearful of supernatural annoyance, used to accompany him. The little old white-coated miller who there ground corn and wheat for his neighbors, whenever he made a particularly early visit to the mill, used to hear it in full operation—the water-wheel dashing bravely, and the old ricketty building clattering to the jar of the stones. Yet the moment his hand touched the latch, or his foot the threshold, all was hushed, save the melancholy drip of water from the dam, or the low gurgle of the small stream eddying amidst willowroots and mossy stones in the ravine below.[4]

This haunted mill has always reminded me of that most beautiful of Scottish ballads, "The Song of the Elfin Miller,"[5] in which fairies are represented as grinding the poor man's grist without toll:—

> Full merrily rings the mill-stone round,
>   Full merrily rings the wheel,
> Full merrily gushes out the grist,—
>   Come, taste my fragrant meal!

[4] As Garrison has observed, Whittier seems to have used this story in his poem, "Birchbrook Mill," written many years later.
[5] Allan Cunningham's poem of that title.

> The miller he's a warldly man,
>   And maun hae double fee;
> So draw the sluice in the churl's dam,
>   And let the stream gae free!

Whoever has seen Great Pond, in the East parish of
Haverhill, has seen one of the very loveliest of the thousand
little lakes or ponds of New England. With its soft slopes
of greenest verdure—its white and sparkling sand-rim—its
southern hem of pine and maple, mirrored, with spray and
leaf, in the glassy water—its graceful hill-sentinels round
about, white with the orchard-bloom of spring, or tasselled
with the corn of autumn—its long sweep of blue waters,
broken here and there by picturesque headlands—it would
seem a spot, of all others, where spirits of evil must shrink,
rebuked and abashed, from the presence of the Beautiful.
Yet here, too, has the shadow of the supernatural fallen. A
lady of my acquaintance, a staid, unimaginative church-
member, states that, a few years ago, she was standing in
the angle formed by two roads, one of which traverses the
pond shore, the other leading over the hill which rises
abruptly from the water. It was a warm summer evening,
just at sunset. She was startled by the appearance of a horse
and cart of the kind used a century ago in New England,
driving rapidly down the steep hillside, and crossing the wall
a few yards before her, without noise, or displacing of a
stone. The driver sat sternly erect, with a fierce countenance;
grasping the reins tightly, and looking neither to the right
nor the left. Behind the cart, and apparently lashed to it,
was a woman of gigantic size, her countenance convulsed
with a blended expression of rage and agony, writhing and
struggling, like Laocoön in the folds of the serpent. Her

head, neck, feet, and arms were naked; wild locks of grey hair streamed back from temples corrugated and darkened. The horrible cavalcade swept by across the street, and disappeared at the margin of the pond.

I have heard many similar stories, but the foregoing may serve as a sample of all. When we consider what the popular belief of New England was no longer than a century and a half ago, it is by no means surprising that something of the old superstition still lingers among us. Our Puritan ancestors were, in their own view of the matter, a sort of advance guard and forlorn hope of Christendom, in its contest with the Bad Angel. The New World, into which they had so valiantly pushed the outposts of the Church militant, was to them, not God's world, but the Devil's. They stood there on their little patch of sanctified territory, like the game-keeper of *Der Freischütz* in the charmed circle[6]—within were prayer and fasting, unmelodious psalmody, and solemn hewing of heretics "before the Lord in Gilgal"; without were "dogs and sorcerers," red children of perdition, Powah wizards, and "the foul fiend." In their grand old wilderness, broken by fair, broad rivers, and dotted with loveliest lakes, hanging with festoons of leaf and vine and flower the steep sides of mountains, whose naked tops rose over the surrounding verdure like altars of a giant world—with its early summer greenness, and the many-colored wonder of its autumn, all glowing as if the rainbows of a summer shower had fallen upon it, under the clear, rich

[6] This story is best known today in Carl Maria von Weber's opera of the same title (1821). He found it in the *Gespensterbuch* of Johann Apel and Friedrich Laun, but he was not the first composer to use it. It may have originated in a Bohemian witchcraft case of the early eighteenth century.

light of a sun, to which the misty day of their cold island was
as moonlight—they saw no beauty, they recognized no holy
revelation. It was to them terrible as the forest which Dante
traversed on his way to the World of Pain. Every advance
step they made was upon the Enemy's territory. And one
has only to read the writings of the two Mathers to perceive
that that enemy was to them no metaphysical abstraction,
no scholastic definition, no figment of a poetical fancy, but
a living, active Reality, alternating between the sublimest
possibilities of evil, and the lowest details of mean mischief;
now a "tricksy spirit," disturbing the good wife's platters or
soiling her new-washed linen, and anon riding the storm-
cloud, and pointing its thunder-bolts; for, as the elder
Mather pertinently inquires, "how else is it that our meet-
ing-houses are burned by the lightning?" What was it, for
instance, but *his* subtlety which, speaking through the lips
of Madam Hutchinson,[7] confuted the "Judges of Israel,"
and put to their wit's end the goodly ministers of the puritan Zion? Was not his evil finger manifested in the con-
tumacious heresy of Roger Williams? Who else gave the
Jesuit missionaries—locusts from the pit as they were—such
a hold on the affections of those very savages who would not
have scrupled to hang the scalp of Father Wilson[8] himself
from their girdles? To the vigilant eye of Puritanism was he
not alike discernible in the light wantonness of the Maypole revellers,[9] beating time with the cloven-foot to the vain

[7] Ann Hutchinson (1591–1643) was banished from the Massachusetts Bay Colony for her antinomian views in 1638.

[8] Probably John Wilson (c. 1591–1667).

[9] The reference is to Thomas Morton's settlement (1625) at
Quincy, Mass. Hawthorne wrote a story about it, "The Maypole of
Merry Mount" (in *Twice-Told Tales*), which later furnished the

music of obscene dances; and the silent, hat-canopied gatherings of the Quakers, "the most melancholy of the sects," as Dr. More[10] calls them? Perilous and glorious was it under these circumstances for such men as Mather and Stoughton[11] to gird up their stout loins and do battle with the unmeasured, all-surrounding Terror. Let no man lightly estimate their spiritual knight-errantry. The heroes of old romance, who went about smiting dragons, lopping giants' heads, and otherwise pleasantly diverting themselves, scarcely deserve mention in comparison with our New England champions, who, trusting not to carnal sword and lance, in a contest with principalities and powers—

> Spirits that live throughout
> Vital in every part, not as frail man,

encountered their enemies with weapons forged by the stern spiritual armorer of Geneva. The life of Cotton Mather is as full of romance as the legends of Ariosto, or the tales of Beltenebros and Florisando in Amadis de Gaul. All about him was enchanted ground—devils glared on him in his "closet wrestlings," portents blazed in the heavens above him, while he, commissioned, and set apart as the watcher and warder, and spiritual champion of "the chosen people," stood ever ready for battle, with open eye and quick ear for the detection of the subtle approaches of the enemy. No

literary foundation for Howard Hanson's opera, *Merry Mount.* John Lothrop Motley's novel, *Merry-Mount*, was published in 1849.

[10] Possibly Nicholas More (?–1689), first chief justice of Pennsylvania, who, though at first close to William Penn, was later removed from office.

[11] Probably William Stoughton (1631–1701), provincial governor of Massachusetts, and involved in the Salem witchcraft trials.

77

wonder is it that the spirits of evil combined against him—
that they beset him as they did of old St. Anthony—that
they shut up the bowels of the General Court against his
long cherished hope of the Presidency of Old Harvard—
that they even had the audacity to lay hands on his anti-
diabolical manuscripts, or that "ye divil that was in ye girl
flewe at and tore" his grand sermon against witches. How
edifying is his account of the young bewitched maiden,
whom he kept in his house for the purpose of making experi-
ments which should satisfy all "obstinate Sadducees"! How
satisfactory to orthodoxy, and confounding to heresy, is the
nice discrimination of "ye divil in ye girl," who was choked
in attempting to read the Catechism, yet found no trouble
with a pestilent Quaker pamphlet,[12] who was quiet and

[12] The Quakers appear to have, at a comparatively early period,
emancipated themselves in a great degree from the grosser superstitions of their times. William Penn indeed had a law in his colony
against witchcraft, but the first trial of a person suspected of this
offence, seems to have opened his eyes to its absurdity. George Fox,
judging from one or two passages in his Journal, appears to have held
the common opinions of the day on the subject, yet when confined in
Doomsdale dungeon, on being told that the place was haunted, and
that the spirits of those who had died there still walked at night in
his room, he replied, "that if all the spirits and devils in hell were
there he was over them in the power of God, and feared no such
thing."

The enemies of the Quakers, in order to account for the power
and influence of their first preachers, accused them of magic and
sorcery. "The Priest of Wakefield," says George Fox (one trusts he
does not allude to our old friend the Vicar), "raised many wicked
slanders upon me, as that I carried bottles with me and made people
drink and that made them follow me: that I rode upon a great black
horse, and was seen in one county upon my black horse in one hour,
and in the same hour in another county four-score miles off." In his
account of the mob which beset him at Walney Island, he says, "when

good-humored when the worthy Doctor was idle, but went into paroxysms of rage when he sat down to indite his diatribes against witches and familiar spirits.

All this is pleasant enough now; we can laugh at the Doctor and his demons: but little matter of laughter was it to the victims on Salem hill—to the prisoners in the jails— to poor Giles Corey, tortured with planks upon his breast, which forced the tongue from his mouth, and his life from his old, palsied body—to bereaved and quaking families— to a whole community priest-ridden and spectre-smitten— gasping in the sick dream of a spiritual night-mare, and given over to believe a lie. We may laugh, for the grotesque is blended with the horrible, but we must also pity and shudder. God be thanked!—the delusion has now measurably vanished. They who confronted that delusion in its own age, disenchanting with strong, clear sense, and sharp ridicule, their spell-bound generation,—the German Wierus, the Italian D'Apone, the English Scott and the New England Calef,[13]—deserve high honors as the benefactors

I came to myself I saw James Lancaster's wife throwing stones at my face, and her husband lying over me to keep off the blows and stones. For the people had persuaded her that I had bewitched her husband." (*Whittier's note*).

[13] Johann Wierus or Weiher (Weyer), also known as Jean de Wier (1515–88) was a German by birth and a disciple of Cornelius Agrippa who became personal physician to the Duke of Cleves. In *De praetigiis daemonum* . . . (Basel, 1563), he opposed persecution of witches. He also wrote *Histoires, disputes et discours des illusions et impostures des diables, des magiciens infames, sorcières et empoissoneurs: des ensorcelez et demoniaques et de la guerison d'icieux: item de la punition que meritent les magiciens, les empoissoneurs et les sorcieres* (1579). He had a great influence on Reginald Scott. For extracts from his writings see Henry Charles Lea, *Materials toward a History of Witchcraft*, ed. Arthur C. Howland (University of Pennsylvania

of their race. They were indeed branded through life as infidels and "damnable Sadducees," by a short-sighted priesthood, who ministered to a credulity which could be so well turned to their advantage, but the truth which they uttered lived after them, and wrought out its appointed work, for it had a divine commission and God speed.

> The oracles are dumb,
> No voice or hideous hum
> Runs through the arched roof in words deceiving;
> Apollo from his shrine
> Can now no more divine,
> With hollow shriek the steep of Delphos leaving.

Dimmer and dimmer, as the generations pass away, this tremendous Terror—this all-pervading espionage of Evil—this well-nigh infinite Haunter and Tempter—this active incarnation of motiveless malignity,—presents itself to the imagination. The once imposing and solemn rite of exorcism has become obsolete in the Church. Men are no longer in any quarter of the world racked or pressed under planks, to extort a confession of diabolical alliance. The heretic now

---

Press, 1939), Vol. II, 490ff. By "D'Apone," Whittier probably means to indicate Pietro d'Abano (c. 1250–c. 1316), Italian physician and philosopher, who, probably because of his sympathy with Arabian authorities, was twice charged by the Inquisition with practicing magic. He was acquitted at his first trial and died before the second had been concluded. The rationalistic *Discoverie of Witchcraft* (1584) by Reginald Scott (?–1599) angered King James I and was burned. Robert Calef (1648–1719) was a Boston merchant who opposed the Mathers on the witchcraft trials; Increase Mather burned his *More Wonders of the Invisible World* (1700) in the Harvard Yard.

laughs to scorn the solemn farce of the Church, which in the name of the All-Merciful formally delivers him over to Satan. Oh, for the sake of abused and long-cheated humanity, let us rejoice that it is so, when we consider how for long, weary centuries the millions of professed Christendom stooped, awe stricken, under the yoke of spiritual and temporal despotism, grinding on from generation to generation in a despair which had passed complaining, because Superstition, in alliance with Tyranny, had filled their upward pathway to Freedom with Shapes of Terror—the spectres of God's wrath to the uttermost, the Fiend and that torment, the smoke of which rises for ever. Through fear of a Satan of the future—a sort of bandog of Priestcraft, held in its leash and ready to be let loose upon the disputers of its authority, —our toiling brothers of past ages have permitted their human task-masters to convert God's beautiful world, so adorned and fitted for the peace and happiness of all, into a great prison-house of suffering, filled with the actual terrors which the imagination of the old poets gave to the realm of Rhadamanthus. And hence, while I would not weaken in the slightest degree the influence of that doctrine of future retribution, the truth of which, reason, revelation and conscience unite in attesting, as the necessary result of the preservation in another state of existence of the soul's individuality and identity, I must, nevertheless, rejoice that the many are no longer willing to permit the few, for their special benefit, to convert our Common Father's heritage into a present hell, where, in return for undeserved suffering and toil uncompensated, they can have gracious and comfortable assurance of release from a future one. Better is the fear of the Lord than the fear of the Devil. Holier and more acceptable the obedience of love and reverence than the

81

submission of slavish terror. The heart which has felt the "beauty of holiness," which has been in some measure attuned to the divine harmony, which now, as of old, in the angel-hymn of the Advent, breathes of "glory to God, peace on earth, and good will to men," in the serene atmosphere of that "perfect love which casteth out fear," smiles at the terrors which throng the sick dreams of the sensual, which draw aside the night-curtains of guilt, and startle with whispers of revenge the oppressor of the poor.

There is a beautiful moral in one of Fouqué's Miniature Romances, "Die Kohlerfamilie." The fierce spectre, which rose, giant-like, in its blood-red mantle, before the selfish and mercenary merchant, ever increasing in size and terror with the growth of evil and impure thought in the mind of the latter, subdued by prayer and penitence, and patient watchfulness over the heart's purity, became a loving and gentle visitation of soft light and meekest melody,—"a beautiful radiance at times hovering and flowing on before the traveller, illuminating the bushes and foliage of the mountain forest—a lustre strange and lovely, such as the soul may conceive, but no words express. He felt its power in the depths of his being—felt it like the mystic breathing of the spirit of God."[14]

[14] Tracey's Translation. (*Whittier's note*).

CHAPTER VI

It is confessed of all that a magician is none other than
Divinorum cultor et interpres, a studious observer and
expounder of divine things.

Sir Walter Raleigh

"Fascination," saith Henry Cornelius Agrippa, in the
fiftieth chapter of his first Book on Occult Philosophy, "is
a binding which comes of the spirit of the witch through
the eyes of him that is bewitched entering to his heart. For
the eye being opened and intent upon any one with a strong
imagination, doth dart its beams, which are the vehiculum
of the spirit, into the eyes of him that is opposite to her,
which tender spirit strikes his eyes, stirs up and wounds his
heart and infects his spirit. Whence Apuleius saith, 'Thy
eyes sliding down through my eyes into my inmost heart,
stirreth up a most vehement burning. And when eyes are
reciprocally intent upon each other, and when rays are
joined to rays, and lights to lights, then the spirit of the one
is joined to that of the other; so are strong ligations made
and vehement loves inflamed." Most true, oh erudite Cornelius! And, taking thy definition of Witchcraft, we sadly
fear it is still practised to a very great extent among us. The
best we can say of it is, that the business seems latterly to
have fallen into younger hands, its victims do not appear

to regard themselves as especial objects of compassion, and neither Church nor State seems inclined to interfere with it.

The old tales of New England witchcraft are familiar to all. I shall therefore speak only of some of the more recent manifestations of glamour and magic which have been vouchsafed to an unbelieving generation, which, as King James lamented in his time, "maintains ye old error of ye Sadducees, ye denying of spirits." I give the incidents in the order in which they occur to my memory.

Some forty years ago on the banks of the pleasant little creek separating Berwick in Maine from Somersworth in N. H., within sight of my mother's home, dwelt a plain, sedate member of the Society of Friends, named Bantum. He passed, throughout a circle of several miles, as a conjuror, and skilful adept in the art of magic. To him resorted farmers who had lost their cattle, matrons whose household gear, silver spoons, and table linen had been stolen, or young maidens whose lovers were absent; and the quiet, meek-spirited old man received them all kindly, put on his huge iron-rimmed spectacles, opened his "conjuring book," which my mother describes as a large clasped volume in strange language and black letter type, and after due reflection and consideration gave the required answers without money and without price. The curious old volume is still in the possession of the conjuror's family. Apparently inconsistent as was this practice of the Black Art[1] with the simplicity and

[1] Whittier is of course very inaccurate in speaking of "Black Art" in connection with this man. He was obviously some sort of "sensitive," and if he practiced magic at all, it was certainly white magic. See my *John Greenleaf Whittier: A Portrait in Paradox* (Oxford University Press, 1967), Appendix A, for a discussion of the problems posed by an accusation of witchcraft brought, almost certainly erroneously, against Whittier's mother and aunt.

truthfulness of his religious profession, I have not been able to learn that he was ever subjected to censure on account of it. It may be that our modern conjuror defended himself on grounds similar to those assumed by the celebrated Knight of Nettesheim, in the preface to his first Book of Magick: "Some," says he, "may crie oute that I teach forbidden Arts, sow the seed of Heresies, offend pious ears, and scandalize excellent wits, that I am a sorcerer, superstitious and devilish, who indeed am a Magician. To whom I answer that a magician doth not among learned men signifie a sorcerer or one that is superstitious or devilish, but a wise man, a priest, a prophet; and that the Sybils prophesied most clearly of Christ; that magicians, as wise men, by the wonderful secrets of the world, knew Christ to be born, and came to worship Him, first of all; and that the name of magicke is received by philosophers, commended by divines, and not unacceptable to the Gospel."

The study of Astrology, and occult philosophy, to which many of the finest minds of the middle ages devoted themselves, without molestation from the Church, was never practised with impunity after the Reformation. The Puritans and Presbyterians, taking the Bible for their rule, "suffered not a witch to live"; and not content with burning the books of those who "used curious arts" after the manner of the Ephesians, they sacrificed the students themselves on the same pile. Hence we hear little of learned and scientific wizards, in New England. One remarkable character of this kind seems, however, to have escaped the vigilance of Puritanism. Dr. Robert Child came to this country about the year 1644, and took up his residence in the Massachusetts colony. He was a man of wealth, and owned plantations at Nashaway, now Lancaster, and at Saco, in Maine. He was skilful in mineralogy and metallurgy; and seems to have spent a good deal of money in searching for mines. He is well known as the author of the first decided movement for liberty of conscience in Massachusetts, his name standing at the head of the famous petition of 1646, for a modification of the laws in respect to religious worship, and complaining in strong terms of the disfranchisement of persons not members of the Church. A tremendous excitement was produced by this remonstrance; clergy and magistrates joined in denouncing it; Dr. Child and his associates were arrested, tried for contempt of government, and heavily fined. The Court, in passing sentence, assured the Doctor that his crime was only equalled by that of Korah and his troop, who rebelled against Moses and Aaron. He resolved to appeal to the Parliament of England, and made arrangements for his departure; but was arrested, and ordered to be kept a prisoner in his own house, until the vessel in which he was to sail had left Boston. He was afterwards imprisoned for a considerable length of time, and, on his release, found means to return to England. The Doctor's trunks were searched by the Puritan authorities, while he was in prison, but it does not appear that they detected the occult studies to which he was addicted; to which lucky circumstance, it is doubtless owing, that the first champion of religious liberty in the New World was not hung for a wizard.

Dr. C. was a graduate of the renowned university of Padua, and had travelled extensively in the Old World. Probably, like Michael Scott,[2] he had

> Learned the art of glammarye
> In Padua beyond the sea;

[2] Michael Scott (1789–1835), Scottish novelist.

86

for I find in the dedication of an English translation of a continental work on astrology and magic, printed in 1651, "at the sign of the Three Bibles," that his "sublime hermeticall and theomagicall lore" is compared to that of Hermes[3] and Agrippa. He is complimented as a master of the mysteries of Rome and Germany; and as one who had pursued his investigations among the philosophers of the Old World, and the Indians of the New, "leaving no stone unturned, the turning whereof might conduce to the discovery of what is occult."

There was still another member of the Friends' Society in Vermont, of the name of Austin, who, in answer, as he supposed, to prayer, and a long-cherished desire to benefit his afflicted fellow-creatures, received, as he believed, a special gift of healing. For several years, applicants from nearly all parts of New England visited him with the story of their sufferings, and praying for a relief, which, it is averred, was in many instances really obtained. Letters from the sick who were unable to visit him, describing their diseases, were sent him, and many are yet living who believe that they were restored miraculously at the precise period of time when Austin was engaged in reading their letters. One of my uncles was commissioned to convey to him a large number of letters from sick persons in his neighborhood. He found the old man sitting in his plain parlor, in the simplest garb of his sect—grave, thoughtful, venerable—a drab-coated Prince Hohenlohe.[4] He received the letters in

[3] Hermes Trismegistus, or Thoth, the Egyptian god of wisdom, to whom the authorship of forty-two sacred works was traditionally attributed. See Longfellow's poem about him.

[4] Prince Alexander Leopold Hohenloe-Waldenburg-Schillingsfürst (1794–1849), German Roman Catholic bishop, under fire from both church and state for his prayer cures.

silence, read them slowly, casting them one after another, upon a large pile of similar epistles in a corner of the apartment.

In the town of Kingston, N. H., there lived a few years ago a family of reputed dealers in magic. There were two poor old sisters who used to frighten the school urchins and "children of a larger growth," as they rode by on their gaunt skeleton horses, strung over with baskets for the Newburyport market. They were aware of the popular notion concerning them, and not unfrequently took advantage of it to levy a sort of blackmail upon their credulous neighbors. An attendant at the funeral of one of these sisters, who when living was about as unsubstantial as Ossian's ghost through which the stars were visible, told me that her coffin was so heavy that four stout men could barely lift it.

A near neighbor of mine thinks she has abundant reason for an unfavorable opinion of the eldest of these sisters. It seems that on one occasion she refused the old woman some trifling request; and that the night following, her infant child appeared, all at once, to be seized upon by some unaccountable terror, crying, beyond even the remarkable capability of babies in that respect, and persisting in working his way under the clothes to the foot of the bed, with a pertinacity and obstinacy which he had never before exhibited. He continued in this way so long, that the mother, who was a shrewd woman, and saw as by intuition into the very gist and marrow of things, began to suspect that the spiteful old basket-maker had crept in through the keyhole and was at that moment by the bed-side, invisible to her, but seen plainly enough by the child, perhaps making faces at him, or pinching him with her claw-like fingers, whenever the poor little fellow was dragged up shrieking and struggling from his retreat. In her prompt, energetic way, she told her husband that the child was bewitched, advising him to get up and load his gun with silver (that being the only metal which can take effect upon witches) and try a shot at the malign intruder. Luckily he had no occasion for such an essay of skill, for the boy instantly became quiet. The inference was, that the malicious old sinner had overheard the mother's proposal, and was afraid to run the risk of its execution.

One can scarcely fail of being reminded of Goethe's remarkable ballad of "The Erl King," in which a father is represented as riding late at night, on a lonely road, with his child in his arms. An evil demon, unseen by the father, makes himself visible to the child, whispers to him, entices him, catches at him; he meanwhile vainly striving to call his father's attention to the annoyer. To the fearful inquiries of his son, the father answers, that he sees only the mist wreath, and the old grey willows, and hears only the sound of the wind in the withered foliage.

> "Mein Vater! Mein Vater! jetzt fasst er mich an!
> Erlkönig hat mir ein Leids getan!"

One of my earliest recollections is that of an old woman residing at Rocks village in Haverhill, about two miles from the place of my nativity, who for many years had borne the unenviable reputation of a witch. She certainly had the look of one—a combination of form, voice, and features, which would have made the fortune of an English witch-finder in the days of Matthew Paris[5] or the Sir John Podgers

[5] Matthew Paris (c. 1200–59), English chronicler and favorite of King Henry III.

of Dickens,[6] and insured her speedy conviction in King James' High Court of Justiciary. She was accused of divers ill doings, such as preventing the cream in her neighbors' churn from becoming butter, and snuffing out candles at huskings and quilting parties.

> She roamed the country far and near,
> Bewitched the children of the peasants;
> Dried up the cows and lamed the deer,
> And sucked the eggs and killed the pheasants.

The poor old woman was at length so sadly annoyed by her unfortunate reputation, that she took the trouble to go before a Justice of the Peace, and made solemn oath that she was a Christian woman and no witch.[7]

[6] Sir John Podgers, a character in *Master Humphrey's Clock*.

[7] I was reminded not long since, of this resort of the poor woman to the law, for her justification from the charge of witchcraft, by the following letter addressed to a distinguished lawyer, some sixty or seventy years ago. The original note is in the hands of one of the descendants of the person to whom it was addressed:—

"Pleas your Worships gentlemen Pray doo have sum charety for me A Poor Distrest man that is become now old and Scars able too muntain my famely at the best and Now Sum Peopel has Raised a Reporte that My Wife is a Witch by which I and my famely must Sartenly Suffer if She Cant be Clerd of the thing and a Stop Poot to the Report for Pepel will not have no Delings with me on the account Pray Gentel men I Beeg the faver of you that one or more of you wood trie her for She is Desiros that She may be tried by all Maner of ways that Ever a Woman was tried so that she can git Clear of the Report

from your Poor and Humble Sarvent
Jeams Moor."

(*Whittier's note*).

Not many years since a sad-visaged, middle-aged man might be seen in the streets of one of our sea-board towns, at times suddenly arrested in the midst of a brisk walk, and fixed motionless for some minutes in the busy thoroughfare. No effort could induce him to stir, until, in his opinion, the spell was removed, and his invisible tormentor suffered him to proceed.[8] He explained his singular detention as the act of a whole family of witches, whom he had unfortunately offended during a visit Down East. It was rumored that the offence consisted in breaking off a matrimonial engagement with the youngest member of the family—a sorceress, perhaps, in more than one sense of the word, like that "winsome wench and walie," in Tam O'Shanter's witch-dance at Kirk Alloway. His only hope was that he should outlive his persecutors; and it is said that at the very hour in which the event took place, he exultingly assured his friends that

[8] Pastor Rutzing, of Cleinau, in Altmark, tells us that the tutor of two young gentlemen, sons of the Count von Reuss, was so beset by an invisible power, when taking a walk with his pupils in the court of the castle of Koestritz, *after* dinner, that "he could by no means walk straight forward, but was hurried away with irresistible vehemence in a sidelong direction." This occurred more than once, so that he was obliged to give up accompanying the young counts in their after-dinner walk.

Cotton Mather attributes the plague of witchcraft in New England in about an equal degree to the Quakers and Indians. The first of the sect who visited Boston, Ann Austin and Mary Fisher, the latter a young girl, were seized upon by Deputy Governor Bellingham in the absence of Gov. Endicott, and shamefully stripped naked for the purpose of ascertaining whether they were witches, with the devil's mark on them. In 1662, Elizabeth Horton and Joan Broksop, two venerable preachers of the sect, were arrested in Boston, charged by Gov. Endicott with being witches, and carried two days' journey into the woods, and left to the tender mercies of Indians and wolves. (*Whittier's note*).

the spell was for ever broken, and that the last of the family of his tormentors was no more.

Some years since, a woman who is still living, in Hillsborough county, New Hampshire, was greatly troubled by witches. On one occasion, having, in company with several others, become bewildered in the woods, while searching for berries, she came to the conclusion that a witch had caused the trouble, and resorted to the expedient of turning her clothing, and that of her companions, wrong side outwards, for the purpose, it seems, of destroying the charm. At another time, one of her hens, probably from sickness, behaving contrary to the old lady's notions of barnyard propriety, was at once declared to be bewitched, and was actually baked alive in an oven, in the expectation that the sorceress, whoever or wherever she might be, would suffer in sympathy with her feathered victim.

When a boy I occasionally met at the house of a relative in an adjoining town, a stout, red-nosed, old farmer, of the neighborhood. A fine tableau he made of a winter's evening, in the red light of the birch-log fire, as he sat for hours watching its progress, with sleepy, half-shut eyes, changing his position only to reach the cider-mug on the shelf near him. Although he seldom opened his lips, save to assent to some remark of his host, or to answer a direct question, yet, at times, when the cider-mug got the better of his taciturnity, he would amuse us with interesting details of his early experiences in "the Ohio country."

There was, however, one chapter in these experiences which he usually held in reserve, and with which "the stranger intermeddled not." He was not willing to run the risk of hearing that, which to him was a frightful reality, turned into ridicule by scoffers and unbelievers. The substance of it, as I received it from one of his neighbors, forms as clever a tale of witchcraft as modern times have produced.

It seems that, when quite a young man, he left his homestead, and, strolling westward, worked his way from place to place until he found himself in one of the old French settlements on the Ohio river. Here he procured employment on the farm of a widow, and being a smart, active fellow, and proving highly serviceable in his department, he rapidly gained favor in the eyes of his employer. Ere long, contrary to the advice of the neighbors, and in spite of somewhat discouraging hints touching certain matrimonial infelicities experienced by the late husband, he resolutely stepped into the dead man's shoes; the mistress became the wife, and the servant was legally promoted to the head of the household.

For a time, matters went on cosily and comfortably enough. He was now lord of the soil; and, as he laid in his crops of corn and potatoes, salted down his pork, and piled up his wood for winter's use, he naturally enough congratulated himself upon his good fortune, and laughed at the sinister forebodings of his neighbors. But, with the long winter months came a change over his "Love's young dream." An evil and mysterious influence seemed to be at work in his affairs. Whatever he did after consulting his wife, or at her suggestion, resulted favorably enough; but all his own schemes and projects were unaccountably marred and defeated. If he bought a horse, it was sure to prove spavined, or wind-broken. His cows either refused to give down their milk, or, giving it, perversely kicked it over. A fine sow which he had bargained for, repaid his partiality by devouring, like Saturn, her own children. By degrees a dark thought forced its way into his mind. Comparing his repeated mischances with the ante-nuptial warnings of his neighbors, he, at last, came to the melancholy conclusion that his wife was a witch! The victim in Motherwell's ballad of the Demon Lady, or the poor fellow in the Arabian Tale,[9] who discovered that he had married a Ghoul in the guise of a young and blooming princess, was scarcely in a more sorrowful predicament. He grew nervous and fretful. Old dismal nursery-stories, and all the witch-lore of boyhood, came back to his memory; and he crept to his bed like a criminal to the gallows, half afraid to fall asleep lest his mysterious companion should take a fancy to transform him into a horse, get him shod at a smithy, and ride him to a witch meeting. And, as if to make the matter worse, his wife's affection seemed to increase, just in proportion as his troubles thickened upon him. She aggravated him with all manner of caresses and endearments. This was the drop too much. The poor husband recoiled from her as from a waking nightmare. His thoughts turned to New England; he longed to see once more the old homestead, with its tall well-sweep, and butternut trees by the road-side; and he sighed amidst the rich bottom lands of his new home, for his father's rocky pasture with its crop of stinted mullens. So, one cold November day, finding himself out of sight and hearing of his wife, he summoned courage to attempt an escape; and resolutely turning his back on the West, plunged into the wilderness towards the sun-rise. After a long and hard journey he reached his birthplace, and was kindly welcomed by his old friends. Keeping a close mouth

[9] Possibly the story of "The Prince and the Ogress," but if so, Whittier's indication of its content is not accurate.

with respect to his unlucky adventure in Ohio, he soon after married one of his schoolmates, and by dint of persevering industry and economy, in a few years found himself in possession of a comfortable home.

But his evil star still lingered above the horizon. One summer evening, on returning from the hay-field, who should meet him but his Witch-wife from Ohio! She came riding up the street on her old white horse, with a pillion behind the saddle. Accosting him in a kindly tone, yet not without something of gentle reproach for his unhandsome desertion of her, she informed him that she had come all the way from Ohio to take him back again.

It was in vain that he pleaded his later engagements; it was in vain that his other wife raised her shrillest remonstrances, not unmingled with expressions of vehement indignation at the revelation of her husband's real position; the Witch-wife was inexorable; go he must, and that speedily. Fully impressed with a belief in her supernatural power of compelling obedience, and perhaps dreading more than witchcraft itself, the effects of the unlucky disclosure on the temper of his New England help-mate, he made a virtue of the necessity of the case, bade good-bye to the latter amidst a perfect hurricane of reproaches, and mounted the white horse with his old wife on the pillion behind him. Of that ride Bürger might have written a counterpart to his Leonore. Two or three years had passed away, bringing no tidings of the unfortunate husband, when he once more made his appearance in his native village. He was not disposed to be very communicative, but for one thing, at least, he seemed willing to express his gratitude. His Ohio wife, having no spell against intermittent fever, had paid the debt of nature, and had left him free; in view of which, his surviving wife, after manifesting a due degree of resentment, consented to take him back to her bed and board, and I could never learn that she had cause to regret her clemency.

CHAPTER VII

> Our superstitions twine
> Each with the next, until a line
> They weave, that through each varied stage
> Runs on from infancy to age,
> Linking the spring with summer weather,
> And chaining youth and years together.

Something of that deeply-wrought superstition of our Scotch and Irish ancestors, embodied in their Banshee and Bodach Glas, the melancholy spectral presage of coming death, beautiful in the melody of Moore and the romance of Scott, still exists in New England. A writer in the N. A. Review of 1832,[1] alluding to the subject says: "Our minds involuntarily turn to the instance in which the early death

---

[1] The only article on occult matters published in *The North American Review* during 1832 seems to be a piece in the January number (Vol. XXXIV, 198–220), based on Charles W. Upham, *Lectures on Witchcraft* . . . and James Thacher, *An Essay on Demonology, Ghosts and Apparitions, and Popular Superstitions,* but no such instance of clairvoyance is included in it.

of one of the brightest sons of genius in this city (Boston) was revealed at the moment of its occurrence to his venerable father, himself sinking under the pressure of infirmity, at a distance from home. We have also heard, on authority which we cannot now question, another instance, in which a lady of no vulgar mind communicated to her friends her impression of the death of a favorite daughter, from whom she had long been separated, and where the event justified the impression."

Two similar instances have occurred in my immediate vicinity. During the late war with Great Britain, a sloop of war was lost on Lake Erie, and among those who perished was Lieut. O——, of Salisbury. On the night of the event, his brother, who had just retired to rest, was startled by a loud, hoarse, gurgling sound, like that produced by the plunging of a heavy mass in water. He left his bed instantly, and declared his conviction that his brother had just been drowned in the lake. A circumstance of the same nature occurred in the case of Capt. B——, of the neighboring town, who was last year drowned near Eastport. The memory, probably, of every reader will recur to some parallel case.

Is it not possible that there is a reality in this? May it not be the result of laws which have hitherto escaped human investigation? May not the spirit, on the eve of its departure, communicate with beloved objects by the simple volition of intense sympathy without the aid of its ordinary medium? Walton, in his life of Dr. Donne, after relating a striking case of this kind, attempts to account for it by supposing the existence of a sympathy of soul—as when one of two lutes in the same apartment is touched, a soft responsive note will be heard from the other. May not the sudden agony of death, intensated by the thought of some dear and distant object of affection, communicate a vibration to the electric chain of mental and physical affinity, strong enough to reach that object, and impress it with an unmistakable sense of its bereavement?

As might be expected, in a community like ours, attempts are not infrequently made to speculate in the supernatural— "to make gain of soothsaying." In the autumn of last year, a "wise woman" dreamed or somnambulized, that a large sum of money, in gold and silver coin, lay buried in the centre of the great swamp in Poplin, N. H., whereupon an immediate search was made for the precious metal. Under the bleak sky of November, in biting frost and sleet-rain, some twenty or more grown men, graduates of our "common schools," and liable, every mother's son of them, to be made deacons, squires, and General Court members, and such other drill-officers as may be requisite in the "march of mind," might be seen delving in grim earnest, breaking the frozen earth, uprooting swamp-maples and hemlocks, and waking, with sledge and crow-bar, unwonted echoes in a solitude which had heretofore only answered to the woodman's axe, or the scream of the wild fowl. The snows of December put an end to their labors; but the yawning excavation still remains, a silent but somewhat expressive commentary upon the "Age of Progress."

Still later, in one of our Atlantic cities, an attempt was made, partially, at least, successful, to form a company for the purpose of digging for money in one of the desolate sandkeys of the West Indies. It appears that some mesmerized "subject," in the course of one of those somnambulic voyages of discovery in which the traveller, like Satan in Chaos:

99

> O'er bog, o'er steep, through straight, rough, dense,
>   or rare,
> With head, hands, wings, or feet, pursues his way,
> And swims, or sinks, or wades, or creeps, or flies,

while peering curiously into the earth's mysteries, chanced to have his eyes gladdened by the sight of a huge chest packed with Spanish coins, the spoil, doubtless, of some rich-freighted argosy, or Carthagena galleon, in the rare days of Queen Elizabeth's Christian buccaneers. Who, after this, shall set limits to Yankee faith in—money-getting?

A curious affair of this kind astonished the worthy citizens of Rye, N. H., last spring. Rye is a small farming and fishing town, looking out upon the broad Atlantic; and, in the summer season, with its green headlands jutting out into the ocean; its fine white beach, relieved in the background by dark green woods, through which peer out the white walls of farmhouses, it is deservedly held in high estimation as a quiet and beautiful place of resort from the unmitigated heats of the island. In the winter and spring its inhabitants are almost entirely left to themselves. In early March, however, of this year, a double sleigh drove to the door of Elder Philbrick, a worthy old gentleman, whose attention is by turns occupied with the duties of a landlord and publican, the oversight and direction of half-a-dozen fishing-smacks, and the untying of knotty texts of scripture. It deposited four of its passengers—three long, solemn-looking men, with hair hanging down around their lank visages "like pounds of candles," and a female figure, closely muffled and veiled. They bespoke lodgings of the Elder, who was not a little puzzled to divine why his guests had chosen such an inappropriate season for their visit. Early the next morning, however, the good man was still more amazed to see the whole party wend their way to the beach, where one of them appeared engaged in performing some mysterious incantation over the veiled figure, moving his hands in a mysterious manner above her head, and describing strange circles in the air before her. They soon returned to their lodgings, conducted the woman to her room, and having borrowed the Elder's shovels and crowbar, immediately commenced digging with great diligence in the spot which had been occupied by the veiled mystery, only abandoning their work as the night closed around them. The same ceremony was acted over again the next morning; and Elder P., deeming it his duty as a Christian man to inquire into the matter, was gravely informed that his visitors were in search of a large sum of money, which the veiled woman had seen in the magnetic sleep, a few feet below the surface of the beach! The search continued for three or four weeks; the muffled Pythoness perversely changing the location of the treasure, now to the right, and anon to the left of the previous day's excavation, wearying alike the souls and bodies of her companions with hope deferred and hard delving. They were at length reluctantly compelled to relinquish their object, and depart sorrowful and heavy at heart, yet firm in their faith that they were leaving behind them a treasure reserved for some more fortunate experimenters in somnambulism and second-sight.

Fortune-telling did not die with Moll Pitcher,[2] the celebrated Lynn Pythoness. There is still living, within a few

[2] A famous psychic of the Lynn-Nahant area, Mass. Whittier wrote a wild, purely fictional account of her in a long poem called *Moll Pitcher* (1831), of which he saved only a fragment, as "Extract from 'A New England Legend,'" in his collected poems. William

miles of my residence, an old colored woman, who during the last twenty years, has been consulted by hundreds of anxious inquirers into the future. Long experience in her profession has given her something of that ready estimate of character, that quick and keen appreciation of the capacity, habits, and wishes of her visitors, which so remarkably distinguished the late famous Madame Le Normand,[3] of Paris. And if that old squalid sorceress, in her cramped Parisian attic, redolent of garlic, and bestrewn with the greasy implements of sorry housewifery, was, as has been affirmed, consulted by such personages as the fair Josephine Beauharnois, and the "Man of Destiny," Napoleon himself, is it strange that the desire to lift the veil of the great mystery before us should overcome, in some degree, our peculiar and most republican prejudice against color, and reconcile us to the disagreeable necessity of looking at Futurity through a black medium?

The excellent Baxter, and other pious men of his day, deprecated in all sincerity and earnestness, the growing disbelief in witchcraft and diabolical agency, fearing that mankind, losing faith in a visible Satan and in the supernatural powers of certain paralytic old women, would diverge into universal skepticism. It is one of the saddest of sights to see these good men standing sentry at the Horn Gate of Dreams,—attempting against most discouraging odds to de-

---

Sloane Kennedy takes a very favorable view of her character in his *John Greenleaf Whittier, The Poet of Freedom* (Funk and Wagnalls, 1892), 278ff., but Upham, Drake, and Alonzo Lewis (*The History of Lynn*, 1829) are much less friendly toward her. See T. R. Garrison's dissertation, pp. 254–55.

[3] Marie Anne Adélaïde Lenormand (1773–1843), who not only functioned as a medium but also wrote on psychic themes.

fend their poor fallacies from profane and irreverent investigation,—painfully pleading doubtful Scripture and still more doubtful tradition, in behalf of detected and convicted superstitions tossed on the sharp horns of ridicule, stretched on the rack of philosophy, or perishing under the exhausted receiver of science. A clearer knowledge of the aspirations, capacities and necessities of the human soul, and of the revelations which the Infinite Spirit makes to it, not only through the senses by the phenomena of outward nature, but by that inward and direct communion, which under different names has been recognized by the devout and thoughtful of every religious sect and philosophy, would have saved them much anxious labor and a good deal of reproach withal in their hopeless championship of error. The witches of Father Baxter, and "the Black Man" of Cotton Mather have vanished; belief in them is no longer possible on the part of sane men. But this mysterious Universe, through which, half veiled in its own shadow, our dim little planet is wheeling, with its star-worlds and thought-wearying spaces, remains. Nature's mighty miracle is still over and around us; and hence awe, wonder and reverence remain to be the inheritance of humanity; still are there beautiful repentances and holy deathbeds, and still over the soul's darkness and confusion rises star-like the great idea of duty. By higher and better influences than the poor spectres of superstition man must henceforth be taught to reverence the Invisible, and in the consciousness of his own weakness and sin and sorrow, to lean with child-like trust on the wisdom and mercy of an overruling Providence.

CHAPTER VIII

Thus saith the Book, "Permit no witch to live,"
　　Hence Massachusetts hath expelled the race,
Connecticut, where swap and dicker thrive,
　　Allows not to their feet a resting-place.
With more of hardihood and less of grace,
　　Vermont receives the sisters grey and lean,
Allows each witch her broomstick flight to trace
　　O'er mighty rocks and mountains dark with green,
Where tempests wake their voice and torrents roar
　　between.

So sang Brainard many years ago. The hospitality of the good people of Vermont is proverbial, and, for aught we know, it may have been extended even to those whom seaboard Puritanism has felt bound to exorcise and cast out by Law and Gospel. But that the evil brood is not entirely extirpated, even in the old Bay State, seems manifest enough.

It is an old and familiar proverb, that a certain malignant personage is always nearest at hand when spoken of; and, in confirmation of this, since my last chapter was written, a

scene of genuine *diablerie* has been enacted in the goodly
and respectable town of Pepperell, in an adjoining county.
There, it seems, is a veritable witch, riding o' nights in this
cold autumnal moonlight, on a spectral white horse, like
that of Dana's Buccaneer,[1] with

> ghostly sides,
> Pale streaming with a cold blue light,

—a steed upon whose silent hoof shoe was never set, unless
by the grim artisans of the infernal smithy. A poor girl,
supposed to be one of her victims, recently died, and on the
night of her death the witch was seen riding hurry-scurry
around the house, not indeed by natural eyesight, but
through the magic spectacles of animal magnetism. A
mesmerized girl was put on the track of an old woman long
suspected of being a little better than she should be. She
found her body lying *without any spirit in it*—the merest
husk and shell imaginable, and following in the track of the
wandering soul, discovered its whereabout. She is at present
grievously afflicting another poor child; and, as is usual with
such evil-disposed characters, has made sad work with the
dairies of her neighbors, bewitching churns and preventing
the butter from "coming"—a peculiarly diabolic feat, which
Burns alludes to in his enumeration of the ill-doings of
"Auld Clootie":

> These kintra wives wi' toil an' pain,
> May plunge an' plunge the kirn in vain,

[1] "The Buccaneer" is probably the best-known single poem by
Richard Henry Dana I (1787–1879), father of the author of *Two
Years Before the Mast*.

> Far, ah, the yellow treasure's ta'en
>   By witching skill.

In this case, however, she has not altogether escaped with impunity, for the red hot tongs being suddenly applied to the refractory cream, a corresponding burn was found the next day on her own "shrunk shank." Upon this fact and the evidence of the somnambulist, some of the good people are half disposed to hang her outright, as an undoubted witch.

The circumstance of the old woman's abandonment of her body during her nocturnal equestrian excursions, reminds us of the hypothesis of the erudite Dr. Jung Silling, in his "Theorie der Geisterkunde." The Doctor professes to believe that the soul in a peculiar state of exaltation may be disengaged from the body, for a short space of time, without the supervention of death, and cites several remarkable instances in support of his belief.

I am reminded of a story somewhat in point. An old strolling woman who, all along the valley of the Piscataqua, was known as a fortune-teller, and was even suspected of witchcraft, called once at my grandfather's house while he was absent. The young girls naturally enough employed her in delineating their future fortunes, but it unluckily chanced that just in the midst of the soothsaying my grandfather's heavy boot-fall was heard on the staircase. All was now consternation, for the stout-hearted, clear-headed old gentleman entertained a very emphatic contempt for all the petty superstitions of his neighborhood and times; and so far as ridicule and sarcasm went, he was as unsparing and merciless toward the pretenders to magic, as Saul was to the "wizards and women with familiar spirits" in his day. The teacup with its occult deposits, so profoundly significant to initiated eyes, was hastily put aside, and the old sorceress, who had some reason for regarding my grandfather as her evil genius, threw herself upon a bed, where she lay for two hours in a kind of trance, defying all efforts to awaken her. At length she started up, and shook back her grey locks from her eyes, declaring that *"she had had a sweet breezing spell!"* Her young questioners took note of the fact that during her seeming sleep, the sky was overcast and wild gusts of wind swept down the river, upsetting wherries, and playing all manner of mad pranks with the marketboats of their brothers coming home from Portsmouth. Is there not something in this to remind one of Lapland wind-making and cloud-compelling Norna?

During the past summer the quiet Shakers of Canterbury, N. H., who profess, in the midst of a sneering generation, to have restored within their family limits the lost innocence and purity of Eden, have, I am told, like our first parents, been troubled with the subtle enemy. Not having forgotten his old tricks, he has once more crept into Paradise. He has been only seen by two or three peculiarly sagacious members of the family; but they have had several thorough hunts for him, the entire community joining with commendable alacrity in the search, and at times very nearly succeeding in capturing him. Once upon the barn they supposed they had him fast, but he escaped the eye of some less vigilant brother or sister, and took refuge under the great stone watering-trough. His cunning saved him; and he still, as my informant states, goes about subjecting the worthy family to divers perplexities and troubles, and new hunts equal to any recorded in the older annals of New England.

One of the last efforts of the lamented Brainard, to whom I am indebted for the motto of this chapter, during the sickness which terminated his life, was a graphic and richly humorous description of the adventures of two sober citizens of Vermont, who in the summer of 1827 dug over the wharves at New-London, Connecticut, in search of buried money. They acted under the direction of an old woman in Vermont, who pretended that the devil had given her a stone by looking through which she could see all the lost treasures of the earth and sea.[2]

The same writer has happily versified a pleasant superstition of the valley of the Connecticut. It is said that shad are conducted from the Gulf of Mexico to the Connecticut by a kind of yankee bogle in the shape of a bird. He makes his appearance annually about a week before the shad, calls them after him, and gives warning to the fishermen to mend their nets.

The Shad Spirit

Now drop the bolt, and securely nail
    The horse-shoe over the door;
'Tis a wise precaution, and if it should fail,
    It never fail'd before.

Know ye the Shepherd that gathers his flock,
    Where the gales of the Equinox blow,
From each unknown reef, and sunken rock
    In the Gulf of Mexico;

While the Monsoons growl, and the trade-winds bark,
    And the watch-dogs of the surge

[2] The name of the poem referred to is "The Money Diggers."

Pursue through the wild waves the ravenous shark,
  That prowls around their charge?

To fair Connecticut's northernmost source,
  O'er sand-bars, rapids, and falls,
The Shad Spirit holds his onward course,
  With the flocks which his whistle calls.

O how shall we know where he went before?
  Will he wander around for ever?
The last year's shad-heads shall shine on the shore,
  To light him up the river.

And well can he tell the very time
  To undertake his task—
When the pork barrel's low he sits on the chine,
  And drums on the empty cask.

The wind is light, and the wave is white,
  With the fleece of the flock that's near:
Like the breath of the breeze, he comes over the seas,
  And faithfully leads them here,

And now he's passed the bolted door,
  Where the rusted horse-shoe clings;
So carry the nets to the nearest shore,
  And take what the Shad Spirit brings.

CHAPTER IX

There is one phase of the supernatural which perhaps more than any other is at the present day manifested among us, growing out of the enthusiasm which not unfrequently attends strong religious feeling and excitement. Thus the state of Trance or Ecstasy, the subject of which sometimes visits in imagination the abodes of blessed spirits, hears ravishing music, and gazes upon Ineffable Glory,—

> Sees distant gates of Eden gleam,
> And does not dream it is a dream,

is not confined to the Methodist camp-ground, but is sometimes among the phenomena of an awakened religious interest in other sects. The doctrine of the second coming of the Messiah, which has been zealously preached in almost all sections of New-England a few years past, has had a powerful influence over the imaginative faculty in its recipients. One of my neighbors, a worthy and estimable man, believes that in the summer of 1838, he saw the "sign of the Son of Man in the heavens" at noon-day—a glorious human form, with the figure 5 directly beneath it, indicating that the great consummation was to be in five years, in 1843. I have alluded to this subject with somewhat of hesitation and delicacy, for I feel it extremely difficult to define the exact point where devotion ends and fanaticism begins. In the beautiful records which Lady Guion, John Woolman, Dr. Payson and Mary Fletcher,[1] have left us of their religious experience, we are compelled to make some allowance for over-wrought feeling and imagination. Bunyan, in his remarkable autobiography, *Grace Abounding*, tells us that he heard devils behind him, and that he kicked at and spurned them; Swedenborg seems, at times, little better than a spiritual Munchausen; Sir Henry Vane, the glorious martyr in the cause of civil and religious freedom, believed himself specially called to bear rule in the millennium; Luther, with true Teutonic vigor, dashed his massive ink-stand in the face of the Annoyer, grimly glaring on him through the stone wall of his cell, being "born," to use his own words, "to fight with devils"; Wesley was beset with invisible house-haunters; George Fox rebuked a witch in

[1] Lady Guion probably indicates Jeanne Marie Bouvier de la Motte-Guyon (1648–1717), French mystical writer, generally called Madame Guyon. See Gamaliel Bradford's psychograph of her in his *Daughters of Eve* (Houghton Mifflin, 1930). John Woolman (1721–72) was the most famous and influential early American Quaker. His *Journal*, now one of the classics of early American literature, was published by Whittier in 1872. Whittier's introduction to it has been reprinted in his *Prose Works*, Vol. II, and in Vol. VII of the collected editions of Whittier's writings. Dr. Payson was possibly Edward Payson (1783–1827), New England Congregational clergyman of wide renown. By "Mary Fletcher," Whittier may mean to indicate Maria Jane Jewsbury Fletcher (Mrs. William Kew Fletcher) (1800–33), who wrote *Phantasmagoria* (1824), *Letters to the Young* (1828), etc.

his meeting,—but are we therefore to shut our eyes to the reality of the spiritual life in these men? For myself, I cannot but treat with some degree of reverence and respect every manifestation of the religious principle, even when it seems to me the reverse of that quiet obedience to simple duty, that sober and "reasonable service" which our Heavenly Father requires at the hands of his children. The excesses and extravagances to which I have alluded, are not the fault of the great subject itself, nor always of the manner, however, objectionable, in which it is presented. The infinite importance of the soul's preparation for the great change which awaits it—the terrible and glorious imagery of the Bible—Heaven's unimaginable bliss, hell's torment unutterable,—the sudden-awakening of a sordid earth-bent soul to the consciousness that broad acres and hoarded coin are but shadows and phantoms, that Eternity and God are realities—the startling inburst of truth upon a hard, dark heart, throwing intolerable light upon its secret sin—the overwhelming contrast of human weakness and guilt with Almighty power and purity—surely in all this there is enough to shake and overawe the strongest mind. Often to minds which have groveled in the very earth, wholly absorbed in sensuality, it carried an instantaneous revelation of the tremendous conditions of their existence. It is to them like the light which shone down upon Saul of Tarsus. They tremble to know of a truth that "a spirit is within them," that life is no longer a mere money-making convenience, that the universe is no longer dead mechanism: even sequences of Nature seem to stretch beyond the limited horizon of time and lose themselves in the Infinite; the simplest phenomena of daily life take a solemn and supernatural character. Is it strange, that such circumstances of intense excitement should sometimes lead to a temporary aberration of intellect? It is indeed painful to witness in a Christian assembly the extravagance and superstitious folly of an Indian powow, or the whirl-dance of the Dervishes of Stamboul. But there is a sadder spectacle than even this. It is to see men regarding with satisfaction such evidences of human weakness, and professing to find in them new proofs of their miserable theory of a Godless universe, and new occasion for sneering at sincere devotion as cant, and humble reverence as fanaticism. Alas! in comparison with such, the wildest and most extravagant enthusiast, who in the midst of his delusion still feels that he is indeed a living soul, and an heir of immortality to whom God speaks from the immensities of His universe, is a sane man. Better is it in a life like ours to be even a howling Dervish or a dancing Shaker, confronting imaginary demon's with Thalaba's talisman of FAITH,[2] than to lose the consciousness of our own spiritual nature, and look upon ourselves as mere brute masses of animal organization—barnacles on a dead universe; looking into the dull grave with no hope beyond it; earth gazing into earth, and saying to corruption, "thou art my father," and to the worm, "thou art my sister."

The preparation of this little volume has been to me a pleasant recreation, a grateful relief from the ordinary task-work of life; a brief turning aside from a heated and dusty highway to the haunted shades and dim grottoes of Fancy:—

A pleasing land of drowsy head it was,
Of dreams that flit before the half-shut eye.

[2] The reference is to Robert Southey's poem, *Thalaba the Destroyer* (1801).

May I not hope that its perusal will afford pleasure to others —making heavy and lonely hours lighter and happier, breaking the sad monotony of the sick chamber, and relieving with innocent amusement the weary treadmill of labor? In a desultory manner I have thrown together such facts in illustration of my subject as chanced to present themselves, with very little regard to order or connexion. It has been no part of my object to apply to these facts the test of philosophical and scientific analysis. I have contented myself with sketching in dim and indistinct outline the great temple of mystery, leaving to others the task of ascertaining whether it is really a solid structure or a palace of cloud-land; and of applying with mathematical accuracy Ezekiel's reed to the walls thereof and the gates thereof. The very nature of my subject has led me, by sudden transitions, from the grave to the gay; from the horrible to the grotesque and ludicrous; and it has been difficult to avoid altogether the appearance of irreverence on the one hand, and of credulity on the other. I am aware that there are graver aspects of the subject than any I have presented, and which are entitled to serious enquiry. For the Supernaturalism of New England and of all other countries is but the exaggeration and distortion of actual fact—a great truth underlies it. It is Nature herself repelling the slanders of the materialist, and vindicating her claim to an informing and all-directing Spirit— the confused and incoherent utterance of her everlasting protest against "the fool who hath said in his heart there is no God."

And, has it never occurred to the thoughtful reader, that the phantasms upon which he has been looking, as he would upon the spectral projections of a showman's magic lantern, are, in fact, but the hieroglyphic representation of spiritual and moral phenomena, which, in a rude age, can only be expressed by significant symbols? In the undefinable power of mind over mind—magnetic forces of attraction and repellency—the mental enslavement of the weak and honest by the strong and evil will,—may we not find a solution of the witchcraft of our ancestors? Are not the passions —perverted from their true purpose, their original harmonies all turned to discord, warring with each other, and leading their victim, like the unhappy one of Scripture, into the fire and the water, and "among the tombs"—fitly described as demons? In the condition of the miser, shivering and starving over his hoarded gold; and of the desperate votary of ambition, hurried away from all the sweet charities and holy affections which make life beautiful and happy; is there nothing to suggest the old idea of possession? Are not memory's chambers always ghost-haunted? Do not our dead, indeed, come back to us, with their looks of unutterable love, or of sorrowful reproach? What is remorse, but the spectre of an evil deed tormenting the guilty one, and following him whithersoever he goes? And what is the fiend himself, but the evil which all men see in others and feel in themselves—a monstrous embodiment of the terrible idea of sin? And may we not conclude with the words of Wilson of Durham:[3] "These sayings of poets, and all their fables, are not to be forgotten; they were not feigned without causes, neither yet continued into the present time, and kept in memory, without consideration."

[3] Thomas Wilson (?–1591), English clergyman, exiled under Mary I, but in favor and in government service under Elizabeth I; dean of Durham Cathedral, 1579.

APPENDICES

APPENDIX A

New England Superstitions,
by John Greenleaf Whittier

—'Tis a history
Handed from ages down; a nurse's tale—
Which children, open-eyed and mouthed, devour;
We learn it and believe.

THALABA

AN ELEGANT WRITER in a late number of *The New England Magazine*[1] has given us an interesting and philosophical essay upon popular superstitions; and made particular allusion to those which may be considered peculiar to, or prevalent in, New England. I cannot but wish that some of our writers (and I know of no one better qualified to perform the tasks than the gentleman I have alluded to) could be induced to embody and illustrate such passages of superstition as may be considered in any way peculiar to the New World. Our fathers had a theory of their own in relation to the invisible worlds—in which they had united, by a most natural process, the wild and extravagant mysteries of their savage neighbors, with the old and common superstitions of their native land; and that stern, gloomy, indefinite awe of an agency of evil, which their peculiar interpretations of the sacred volume had inspired; a theory, which mingled with and had a practical effect upon their habits and dis-

[1] W. B. O. Peabody, "New-England Superstitions," *New England Magazine*, IV (1833), 139–53. Whittier's own "Passaconaway" was in the same (February) number.

positions—which threw a veil of mystery over the plainest passages of the great laws of the universe—which gave a constraint and an awe to their intercourse with one another—agitating the whole community with signs and wonders, and dark marvels, poisoning the fountains of education and constituting a part of their religion.

The principal relics of these ancient superstitions, which still linger with us, may be classed under the following heads:

I. *Haunted Houses.* By which is not always understood the actual appearance of a spirit from the dead; but, not unfrequently, a supernatural disturbance—noises in the deep midnight, the revelling of evil demons, etc.

I have heard but little of haunted houses in this vicinity for some time past. Our Yankee thrift, in truth, does not often allow us to keep houses for the accommodation of such ghostly tenants as never pay for their lodgings. One of my neighbors formerly complained a good deal of the disturbing revels which ghosts or witches nightly got up under his roof. All night long he could hear a dance moving lightly to the tune of some infernal melody:

> Where hornpipes, jigs, strathspeys and reels
> Put life and mettle in the heels

of the unseen revelers. Latterly, however, I learn that his tormentors have given him a respite.

II. *Ghosts.* The appearance of a departed friend or enemy; a visible similitude of the dead, revealed to the living only upon some extraordinary contingency; to publish like that of "Buried Denmark," some "foul and most unnatural murder" or injury; to settle without fee disputes between the heirs of the dead man's property, and for various other "wicked or charitable purposes."

III. *Witches*. Including male and female under the same general term. This class of worthies is getting very much out of repute. In the county of Essex, which was formerly their headquarters, there is not a single survivor, worthy of the name; although we have many most devout believers in their potency. Kingston, New Hampshire, has been somewhat celebrated for a family of witches. Two elderly sisters used, a few years since, to be seen winding their way to market, with a few small baskets of their own manufacture, mounted on horses as lean as their skeleton riders, the objects of great terror to all the urchins of the street. They were evil, malicious, malignant, and their appearance involuntarily reminded one of Otway's famous description in his *Orphan*:

> "I spied a withered hag with age grown double,
> Picking dry sticks, and mumbling to herself;
> Her eyes with scalding rheum were galled and red,
> Cold palsy shook her head, her hands seemed withered,
> And on her crooked shoulders, had she wrapped
> The tattered remnants of an old striped hanging,
> Which served to keep her carcass from the cold."

They are now, I believe, both dead. A person who attended the funeral of one of them told me, with great gravity, that the coffin of her who, when living, was seemingly as insubstantial as the ghosts of Ossian, through which the stars were visible, was at first so heavy that eight stout men could not raise it; but that after waiting a while for the *spell* to be removed, it could be easily taken up by a single man.

IV. *Fortune-telling.* This is still considerably practiced, not so much, however, by the professed disciples of astrology and palmistry, as by the younger classes of our inland community. It is usually called *trying projects,* very much like those described by Burns, in his inimitable Halloween.

V. *Warnings of Death or Disaster.* This species of superstition is completely inwrought. It has most successfully resisted the operations of science and philosophy.

A very honest and intelligent neighbor of mine, once told me that at the precise moment when his brother was drowned in the Merrimac, many miles distant, he felt a sudden and painful sensation—a death-like chill upon his heart, such as he had never before experienced. I have heard many similar relations. Those who have read Walton's life of Donne will recollect the theory of that quaint and excellent old author on this subject, that there is a sympathy of soul—an electric chain of mental affinity—upon which the emotions of one spirit thrill and tremble even to another.

VI. *Spectres.* I use this term in the sense in which it was made to apply, during the memorable era of 1692, to the appearance or phantom of a living person, who, at the time of its visitation, is known to be absent.[2] Such appearances are suppose to denote the speedy death of the person whom they represent.

[2] "Spectre" is generally considered a synonym for "ghost." OED gives no support to Whittier's notion that it must be the apparition of a *living* person.

A widow lady, residing in an adjoining town, is clearly convinced that she saw the spectre of her daughter a little time before her death, yet when she was in perfect health. It crossed the room within a few feet of the mother, and in broad daylight. She spoke; but no answer was returned; the countenance of the apparition was fixed and sorrowful. The daughter was at the time absent on a visit to a friend.

VII. *Supposed Preternatural Appearances.* Unconnected with any circumstances peculiar to those who witness them; lights dancing in lonely places and graveyards, meteors, etc. etc. These are usually denominated *sights.*

I have listened, hour after hour, of a winter's evening, to minute descriptions of these appearances. A much-lamented friend of mine—a sober and intelligent farmer—once informed me, that, while engaged in sledding rails for his spring fence, many years since, his team suddenly stood still, apparently unable to proceed. It was a night of cold, clear moonshine; the path was smooth and slippery as glass; and the pause made about midway in the descent of a hill. He examined the runners on all sides, but no obstruction was apparent. He lifted up the runners in front, and urged forward his oxen at the same time; the cattle exerted their whole strength—the very bows of their yoke cracked with the effort; but the sled remained immovable, as if bedded in a solid rock. After repeated trials had been made, and the farmer was on the point of leaving his sled for the night, a sharp report like that of a pistol was heard—a strong blaze of fire enveloped the whole team; and the sled instantly glided down the declivity with a speed which greatly embarrassed the oxen, which but a moment before had in vain endeavored to move it.

The farmer had never probably read Coleridge's poetical description of a somewhat similar detention of the ship of the "Ancient Mariner," which, held by the demon, in the teeth of the wind, kept swaying and struggling

> Backwards and forwards, half her length,
> With a short, uneasy motion;

and which, when released at last,

> Like a pawing horse set free,
> Sprang forth with sudden bound;

yet the *experimentum crucis*, whereby he attempted to ascertain the cause of such an extraordinary circumstance, led him to ascribe it to witchcraft, or some other supernatural agency. There were facts to be explained, which, in his opinion, could only refer themselves to such a cause.

A pond in my vicinity has been somewhat celebrated for its "sights and marvels." A middle-aged lady of good intelligence, residing near it, states, that one summer evening, between day-light and dark, while standing by the side of the highway leading along the margin of the pond, she was startled by the appearance of a horse, attached to an old-fashioned cart, and driven by an elderly man, plunging at full speed down the hill which rises abruptly from the water, and over a rough pasture where it would seem impossible for a vehicle to be conveyed. It passed swiftly and noiselessly over the high wall bounding the pasture without displacing a stone, and crossed the street within a few yards of the astonished looker-on. Behind the cart, and bound to it by a strong rope, fastened to her wrists, a woman of gigantic stature was dragged furiously onward, writhing like Laocoön in the clasp of the serpent. Her feet, head, and arms were naked; and grey locks of wild hair streamed back from temples corrugated and darkened. The horrible cavalcade swept by, and disappeared in the thick swamp which touches the western extremity of the pond.

I could mention half a dozen other places within a few miles of my residence, equally celebrated for the "unco" sights and sounds which have been seen or heard near them. The Devil's Den, in Chester, N. H., is among the most prominent in this respect. How his satanic majesty came in possession of it, I have never been able to ascertain; but that it is a favorite resort of his is incontestably proved by the fact that he always keeps a smooth foot-track to its entrance, whether in summer or winter. The following rhymes, if they answer no other purpose, will serve to show that the place and its legend are enjoying as comfortable a chance of immortality as Yankee poetry can give them.

> The moon is bright on the rocky hill,
> But its dwarfish pines rise gloomily still,—
> Fixed, motionless forms in the silent air,
> The moonlight is on them, but darkness is there.
> The drowsy flap of the owlet's wing,
> And the stream's low gush from its hidden spring,
> And the passing breeze, in its flight betrayed
> By the timid shiver of leaf and blade,
> Half like a sigh and half a moan,
> The ear of the listener catches alone.
>
> A dim cave yawns in the rude hill-side
> Like the jaws of a monster opened wide,
> Where a few wild bushes of thorn and fern

Their leaves from the breath of the night-air turn;
And half with the twining foliage cover
The mouth of that shadowy cavern over:—
Above it, the rock hangs gloomy and high,
Like a rent in the blue of the beautiful sky,
Which seems, as it opens on either hand,
Like some bright sea leaving a desolate land.

Below it, a stream on its bed of stone
From a rift in the rock comes hurrying down,
Telling forever the same wild tale
Of its loftier home to the lowly vale:
And over its waters an oak is bending,
Its boughs like a skeleton's arms extending,—
A naked tree, by the lightning shorn,
With its trunk all bare and its branches torn;
And the rocks beneath it, blackened and rent,
Tell where the bolt of the thunder went.

'Tis said that this cave is an evil place
The chosen haunt of the fallen race—
That the midnight traveller oft hath seen
A red flame tremble its jaws between,
And lighten and quiver the boughs among,
Like the fiery play of a serpent's tongue;
That sounds of fear from its chambers swell—
The ghostly gibber,—the fiendish yell;
That bodiless hands at its entrance wave,—
And hence they have named it the Demon's Cave!

The fears of man to this place have lent
A terror which Nature never meant;—
For who hath wandered, with curious eye
This dim and shadowy cavern by,

And known, in the sun or star-light, aught
Which might not beseem so lovely a spot,—
The stealthy fox, and the shy raccoon—
The night-bird's wing in the shining moon—
The frog's low croak; and, upon the hill,
The steady chant of the whippoorwill?

Yet is there something to fancy dear
In this silent cave and its lingering fear,—
Something which tells of another age,
Of the wizard's wand, and the Sybil's page,
Of the fairy ring and the Haunted glen,
And the restless phantoms of murdered men:
The granddame's tale, and the nurse's song—
The dreams of childhood remembered long;
And I love even now to list the tale
Of the Demon's Cave, and its haunted vale.[3]

One of the most striking instances of the effects of a disordered imagination recently occurred in this vicinity. The following are the facts:

In September, 1831, a worthy and highly esteemed inhabitant of this town died suddenly on the bridge over the Merrimac, by the bursting of a blood-vessel. It was just at day-break, when he was engaged with another person in raising the draw of the bridge for the passage of a sloop. The suddenness of the event; the excellent character of the deceased; and, above all, a vague rumor, that some extraordinary disclosure was to be made, drew together a large concourse at the funeral. After the solemn services were

[3] The poem, "The Demon's Cave," a good example of Whittier's early, most exuberant manner, was published in *The New England Review*, July 25, 1831.

concluded, Thomas, the brother of the dead man,—himself a most exemplary Christian,—rose up, and desired to relate some particulars concerning the death of his brother. He then stated—and his manner calm, solemn, impressive—that, more than a month previous to his death, his brother had told him, that his feelings had been painfully disturbed by seeing, at different times, on the bridge, a quantity of human blood; that sometimes while he was gazing upon it, it suddenly disappeared, as if removed by an invisible hand; that it lay thick and dark amidst the straw and litter; that, many times, in the dusk of the evening, he had seen a vessel coming down the river, which vanished just as it reached the draw; and that, at the same time, he had heard a voice calling in a faint and lamentable tone—"I am dying" and that the voice sounded like his own; that then he knew that the vision was for him, and that his hour of departure was at hand. Thomas, moreover, stated that, a few days before the melancholy event took place, his brother, after assuring him that he would be called upon to testify to the accounts which he had given of the vision on the bridge, told him that he had actually seen the same vessel go up the river, whose spectral image he had seen in his vision, and that, when it returned, the fatal fulfilment would take place; that, night after night, he had heard what seemed to him the sound of the horn from that vessel, calling for the raising of the draw, and that it was to him very solemn and awful. "You all know," continued the narrator, "how my Brother died, that he died fulfilling the vision, that his blood lies even now upon the bridge, as *he* saw it before his death, and that his last words were heard by the captain of the vessel— 'I am dying!' "

There was something in the circumstances of this narration—the church crowded with faces bent earnestly on the speaker—the evident sincerity, and deep solemnity of the narrator—and the fearful character of his communication—while the yet unburied corpse of his brother lay before him—which was calculated to revive every latent feeling of superstition; and to overpower, at least for the moment, the convictions of reason and the arguments of philosophy.

It is altogether foreign to my purpose to enter into any deliberate analysis of the nature of these superstitions. I have briefly alluded to a few instances, of my own neighborhood and times, for the purpose of showing that, even in our enlightened age and community, the delusions of the past still linger around us; and that there is no lack of materials for an amusing and not uninstructing work of the character I have already mentioned in the beginning of this article.

APPENDIX B

Nathaniel Hawthorne's Review

of *The Supernaturalism of New England*[1]

MR. WHITTIER'S LITERARY NAME has been little other than
an accident of exertions directed to practical and unselfish
purposes—a wayside flower which he has hardly spared the
time to gather. In the dedication of this little volume to his
sister, he well expresses the feeling of relief, and almost
self-reproachful enjoyment, with which he turns aside from
his "long, harsh strife with strong-willed men," to converse
with ghosts and witches, and all such legendary shadows.
We doubt not, he will return to the battle of his life with
so much the more vigor, for this brief relaxation; but we are
bound to say, that, if he could have more entirely thrown off
the mental habit of a man writing under a stern sense of
duty, he might have succeeded better in such a labor of love
and idleness, as the present. In spite of himself, Mr. Whit-

---

[1] Hawthorne's review appeared in *The Literary World*, I (1847),
247–48. The present reprint follows Randall Stewart's text in his
"Two Unpublished Reviews by Hawthorne," *New England Quarterly*,
IX (1936), 504–509. Stewart checked the manuscript in the New
York Public Library and corrected several typographical errors.

tier stoops to the theme with the austere dignity of a schoolmaster at his amusements; a condescension that may seem exaggerated, when we consider that the subject will probably retain a human interest, long after his more earnest efforts shall have lost their importance in the progress of society.

In the first chapter of this book, there are some good remarks on the spiritual tendencies that lie beneath the earthy surface of the Yankee character. Such spirituality certainly does exist; but we cannot perceive that its indications are, or ever have been, so peculiar as to form any system that may come fairly under the title of New England Supernaturalism. The contrary is rather remarkably the fact; the forest-life of the first settlers, and their intercourse with the Indians, have really engrafted nothing upon the mythology which they brought with them from England—at least, we know of nothing, though Mr. Whittier intimates that these circumstances did modify their English superstitions. We should naturally look for something duskier and grander in the ghostly legends of a wild country, than could be expected in a state of society where even dreams are covered with the dust of old conventionalisms. But, if there be any peculiarity, it is, that our superstitions have a more sordid, grimy, and material aspect, than they bore in the clime from which they were transplanted. A New England ghost does not elevate us into a spiritual region; he hints at no mysteries beyond the grave, nor seems to possess any valuable information on subjects of that nature. He throws aside even his shroud, puts on the coat and breeches of the times, and takes up the flesh-and-blood business of life, at the very point where he dropt it at his decease. He so mingles with daily life, that we scarcely perceive him to be a ghost at all.[2] If he indeed comes from the spiritual world, it is because he has been ejected with disgrace, on account of the essential and inveterate earthiness of his substance.

This characteristic of a New England ghost-story should by all means be retained; else the legend will lose its truth. Mr. Whittier has sometimes caught the just effect, but occasionally allows it to escape, by aiming at effects which are inconsistent with the one alluded to. He has made a fine ballad of the "New Wife and the Old":[3]—its only defect is, indeed, that he has made it too fine, at the sacrifice of the homeliness which was its essence. His style, in fact, throughout the volume, has not quite the simplicity that the theme requires; it sparkles a little too much. The proper tone for these legends is, of course, that of the fireside narrative, refined and clarified to whatever degrees the writer pleases, but still as simple as the Bible—as simple as the babble of an old woman to her grandchild, as they sit in the smoky glow of a deep chimney-corner. Above all, the narrator should have faith, for the time being. If he cannot believe his ghost-story while he is telling it, he had better leave the task to somebody else. Now, Mr. Whittier never fails to express his incredulity either before or after the narrative, and often in the midst of it. It is a matter of conscience with him to do so.

One other criticism must be allowed us. Mr. Whittier has

[2] At this point Hawthorne wrote, and marked out, the following sentence: "Such legends do not elevate us into the spiritual world— they degrade the latter into our own actual sphere." (*Stewart's note*).

[3] "I remember hearing the story, when a child, from a venerable family visitant" (*Stewart's note*, presumably from Whittier's manuscript, though no explanation is added).

read too much. He talks too learnedly about the "Ahriman of the Parsee, the Pluto of the Roman mythology, the Devil of the Jew and Christian, the Shitan of the Mussulman, the Machinito of the Indian"; and quotes some black letter mystic or modern poet on every page. There is nothing in his treatment of the subject that requires such an array of authorities, nor any such depth in the well of his philosophy, that we can descend into it only by a flight of steps, constructed out of old folio volumes.

But, how much easier it is to censure than to praise, even where the merits greatly outweigh the defects! We conclude, with the frank admission that we like the book, and look upon it as no unworthy contribution from a poet to that species of literature which only a poet should meddle with. We hope to see more of him, in this, or some other congenial sphere. There are many legends still to be gathered, especially along the sea-board of New England—and those, too, we think, more original, and more susceptible of poetic illustration, than these rural superstitions.

For this edition of *The Supernaturalism of New England,* the types of two distinguished American designers were combined.

The text is set in ten-point Linotype Electra, an original typeface by W. A. Dwiggins (1880–1956), and the display type is Deepdene, one of the most distinctive typefaces cut by Frederic W. Goudy (1885–1947).

Both faces have a crisp, calligraphic quality and an artistic beauty that make them particularly appropriate companions.

The paper on which this book is printed bears the watermark of the University of Oklahoma Press and is designed to have an effective life of over three hundred years.

UNIVERSITY OF OKLAHOMA PRESS

NORMAN